THE PHILLIPS GUIDE TO
ENGLISH
PORCELAIN
of the 18th and 19th Centuries

Published 1989 by Merehurst Press
Ferry House,
51-57 Lacy Road, Putney,
London, SW15 1PR

© Text copyright John Sandon 1989
© Copyright Merehurst Press 1989
By arrangement with Dunestyle Publishing Ltd.

Co-published in the United States of America by
Riverside Book Company, Inc.;
250 West 57th Street;
New York, NY 10107

© **Pictures**   Phillips Fine Art Auctioneers
Edited by   Emma Sinclair Webb
Editorial Director   Megra Mitchell
Art Director   John Strange
Typeset by   O'Reilly Clark (London)
Separations by   Chroma Graphics (Singapore)
Designed by   Strange Design Associates

Printed in Italy by New Interlitho spa

ISBN 1-85391-061-9

THE PHILLIPS GUIDE TO

ENGLISH

PORCELAIN

of the 18th and 19th Centuries

John Sandon

MEREHURST PRESS
— LONDON —

Contents

*A cup and saucer of c.1835,
marked only with a pattern number but
exactly matching the Grainger factory
pattern book.* Worcester Royal Porcelain
Company.

Author's Note

Although this book was written in just a few months of feverish activity, it is the culmination of a lifetime's love of English porcelain. I wanted to produce the kind of book which I needed when I started out in my career fifteen years ago as a junior cataloguer in Phillips' ceramics department. From my father I inherited a keen interest and a certain knowledge of Worcester porcelain, but I had to learn about the entire field of English as well as Continental and Oriental porcelain. Working alongside John Matthews and Jo Marshall I was able to build on my enthusiasm, and their patient guidance helped me to understand not only the wares themselves but the market trends which affect the value of the vast array of porcelain which passes through our hands.

Having progressed to become director of the porcelain department I am now teaching my own junior cataloguers, while at the same time through my various lecture and 'Roadshow' activities I find I am continually being asked for guidance by novice collectors and enthusiasts wishing to gain an understanding of porcelain. In this book I have tried not merely to repeat the names, dates and facts which can be obtained from any number of specialist books. These books, on which I rely, are listed in appendix I. Instead I have attempted to discuss the history and development of English porcelain as if I were presenting a lecture to a group of interested beginners, giving the sort of essential advice on which a serious collector can build. The photographs which make such a project possible have been selected from the many thousands of pieces which have passed through my department over the years, and therefore this is a very personal choice which I hope will illustrate clearly the various points which are discussed.

I am fortunate to have been able to rely on the skills of Chris Halton, the senior photographer at Phillips who has taken the vast majority of the photographs used in this book. Knowing how difficult it is to photograph fine porcelain effectively, I am sure that his photographs will speak for themselves, and through his patience many details can be seen clearly which would not be evident otherwise. Other photographs have been kindly provided by my father Henry Sandon, taken for him while he was curator of the Dyson Perrins Museum in Worcester. My father's help, not only during the production of this book but over twenty years' learning about porcelain, deserves the greatest possible recognition and is reflected in every page of this book. My thanks also go to my wife, Kristin, who not only typed the manuscript but gave me the encouragement needed to sit down and put into words the knowledge which I have gained over the years. Also I am grateful to Michael Poulson for his help and advice at every stage, especially in editing my text.

Principally, though, my thanks go to the staff of Phillips for all manner of assistance in the gathering together of the photographs used in this book, and especially Jo Marshall for her friendship and support ever since I joined the porcelain department. Finally, I hope that you will get as much enjoyment out of using this book as I have had in gathering all my thoughts together to write it.

John Sandon

Chapter One
The Origins of English Porcelain

When porcelain first arrived in Europe it was treasured. The Chinese invention was so far removed from European domestic pottery that it seemed almost mystical. Besides being thin, pure white, hard and durable, it had above all a magic property that made all the difference – it was translucent. Light could be seen through it like opaque glass, only it was stronger and more usable. The name derives from the Italian *porcellana*, or 'little pig', a type of fine seashell to which the material bore a resemblance. Little wonder that the courts and wealthy merchants in Holland, Italy and England prized what little could be obtained through trade via the Middle East. By the beginning of the sixteenth century we find Chinese porcelain mounted in precious metal by Renaissance goldsmiths and set with gems. It featured prominently in still life paintings and scenes of banquets commissioned to represent their patron's wealth, for it was, at this time, too rare and valuable to eat off. References in English literature to 'porseland' or 'porcelanas' emphasize how costly this material was. Porcelain was very scarce and imitations were keenly sought. There would be great rewards for any European potter who could master a technique to reproduce the whiteness and translucency of the original.

Italy led the way with *maiolica*, the name given to earthenware which was coloured white by the addition of tin oxide to the glaze. It looked like porcelain at first sight, but when chipped or broken the red pottery clay inside was revealed. Apart from an experimental and uneconomic attempt by potters working for the Medici family in the sixteenth century to make a porcellaneous ware which could survive the intense heat of the kiln, tin-glazed earthenware was the only white material which could be made in Europe until the end of the seventeenth century. During this time the quality and quantity of imported Chinese porcelain greatly increased, and serious competition developed between potters and the merchants who imported Chinese wares.

In the early 1980s explorations of a shipwreck in the South China Sea yielded a complete cargo of Chinese porcelain destined for Europe. Sunk in the 1640s, this was an earlier and less publicized find than the 'Nanking Cargo' discovered a few years later, but it showed the extensive range of blue and white porcelain which was being shipped, in quantity, through Holland and ultimately arriving in the England of Charles I and Cromwell.

The large sets of jars and vases and the circular dishes known as 'chargers' could be faithfully copied, particularly in Holland and in Germany, in their sophisticated tin-glazed earthenwares. Known in Germany as *Fayence* and in Holland as 'Delft', after the town where so much was manufactured, the wares were thin and finely painted,

ABOVE *A Chinese porcelain bowl recovered from a ship sunk in 1743 in the South China Seas, on its way to Europe. 16.5 cm (6½ in) diameter.* Henry Sandon Collection.

LEFT *A Berlin fayence* Schnabelkanne *in tin-glazed earthenware copying Chinese porcelain, dated 1712, 37 cm (14½ in).*

ABOVE *A Japanese dish made for export and bearing the emblem of the Dutch East India Company which was responsible for most of the trade in oriental porcelain during the seventeenth and eighteenth centuries; 28 cm (11 in), c.1665.*

BELOW *A Chinese puzzle jug, the shape copied from English delftware, painted in* famille verte *and made for export early in the eighteenth century.*

but they lacked the two important qualities which distinguished the Chinese. They were far too soft and would never show light through the tin-glazed pottery.

As early as the sixteenth century Dutch potters began to settle in England, where they were granted royal patents to manufacture tin-glazed pottery. Initially, the potters set up in East Anglia, but were soon established in London, and their products were called delftware after the Dutch town from where the material had been imported until then. English delft in the seventeenth century was more heavily influenced by contemporary metalwork shapes than Chinese porcelain, although by the end of the century plates and dishes exactly copying late Ming blue and white Chinese porcelain were produced in London and at Brislington near Bristol.

Gradually, though, as more and more Chinese porcelain arrived in England, the delft potters had to adapt to changing fashion. Those who could afford it ate off Chinese porcelain and, more importantly, drank tea from Chinese teapots. Tea drinking became a very important social event and the gentry of the day competed with one another to be able to serve their tea in the richest and most splendid services. Chinese porcelain arrived in Europe packed in tea and sold for very high prices at auctions in London and at the ports where the cargoes were unloaded. The custom of drinking tea required two new shapes unknown in English ceramics: a teapot for brewing the leaves and small handleless cups, known as teabowls, which rested on saucers. These had to come into direct contact with boiling water to brew the tea, which posed no problem to the Chinese hard porcelain. English delft teapots, however, were of a much softer material and, as likely as not, would crack when hot liquid was poured in. Consequently few delft teawares survive. To overcome this problem the English adopted a new method of making tea. Instead of pouring hot water directly into the cold teapot, they swirled not quite boiling water in it to 'warm the pot'. They also put milk into the teabowls before the tea, to cool the initial impact of the hot liquid. Both of these habits continue in most English households today. It is interesting to think that the way we make tea today is a tradition that survives from the days when English teawares were more fragile.

Chinese porcelain, throughout Europe, was infinitely better than locally-made pottery. Even when the stonewares of Germany and London could be made thin enough for tea drinking, they were brown or drab and lacked the whiteness of porcelain. In Staffordshire late in the seventeenth century the Elers brothers made a red unglazed stoneware which was thin and reasonably strong, similar to redwares made in Holland and copying, once again, imported Chinese *Yi Hsing* stonewares. Sadly, this could not be produced economically at that time and the buying public preferred the white porcelain anyway. Demand for Chinese services, although costly, continued to grow and earned great sums for the Dutch East India company, which was almost single-handedly responsible for trade with the Far East.

In spite of the cost, the English noblemen were perfectly

prepared to wait while a special porcelain service was manufactured
for them in China and shipped in the private cargo of an East
Indiaman, weighted down with silk and spices, as well as tea. One
such service is illustrated here. In around 1730 the Grantham family
would have sent a drawing of their coat of arms to China to be copied
onto the porcelain, together with a border design chosen from a
pattern book kept by the merchants. The ship which delivered the
order to China would collect the finished service on its next visit to
Canton many months later. Imagine the pride of the lady of the
household as she served tea to her guests in a set for which she had
waited perhaps two years! The shapes are partly Chinese –
particularly the covered sugar bowl – while the tea canister is copied
directly from an English silver shape originally sent to China as a
prototype. Geoffrey Godden, in his excellent book *Oriental Export
Market Porcelain* details many instances of this trade, where European
shapes or patterns were sent to China for copying. A very good
example is the puzzle jug, illustrated opposite, made in Chinese
famille verte porcelain, but directly reproducing an English delftware
jug of roughly similar date. Eighteenth-century copies are known of a
great range of English porcelain vessels which were produced,
presumably more cheaply, by the Chinese.

ABOVE *A Chinese tea service painted in*
famille rose *with the arms of Grantham;*
Yongzheng, c.*1730.*

This overlap of ideas between Chinese and European porcelain makes a fascinating area of collecting. While it is possible to find all sorts of English shapes in Chinese porcelain, usually highly priced today, the Chinese prototypes of many English copies can be picked up very reasonably; they are usually far cheaper than the English reproductions which are fully discussed in Chapter 3. In the meantime it is worth mentioning a very important and also very confusing class of porcelain wares occasionally encountered – Chinese porcelain exported to England to be decorated.

Because of its uniqueness and the beauty of the material, much Chinese porcelain sent to Europe was without any decoration at all. Plain white cups and saucers, particularly with embossed flowering prunus sprigs, were popular early in the eighteenth century. Some of these were subsequently enamelled by china painters working in Europe. Fairly crude enamelling, mostly in red and green, was added in Holland, while in Germany in around 1730, some of the finest glass and porcelain painters used white Chinese porcelain as the base for superb landscapes, often in black monochrome – known as *schwarzlot*.

In England, some crude painting was added in the early eighteenth century to brown glazed Chinese porcelain and red stonewares. Much finer work dates from the 1750s when thin white Chinese tewares were painted in London in a purely European style. Exotic birds, scenes from fables and from the Italian comedy and bouquets of colourful flowers and insects were painted by enamelling workshops such as the studios of James Giles Snr, in Kentish Town, London. It was probably in the Giles workshop that the teapot illustrated opposite was painted. The porcelain is Chinese, although the subject of classical ruins in a peculiar bright green monochrome is very much an English style, found also on some of the earliest porcelain made in London. Some Chinese porcelain seems to have been painted in England with direct copies of Chinese patterns and other oriental style designs. Naturally these are very difficult to recognize but are quite interesting when they can be linked up to contemporary English porcelain painting.

The secret of making porcelain was acquired from China at a fairly early date, but unfortunately the necessary raw materials, in particular china clays known as kaolins, were not known in Europe in the seventeenth century. Many people experimented to perfect a satisfactory copy which would be not only white and translucent, but which could also be manufactured economically. In the 1680s John Dwight, a stoneware potter in London, was granted a patent for making what he called porcelain, but it is considered unlikely that he was ever successful enough to sell any of this ware. Instead it is France who claims the credit for the first manufacturers able to make porcelain in Europe on a reliable and profitable basis. By the end of the seventeenth century a creamy-coloured porcelain was being made at Rouen, and soon afterwards the factory at St. Cloud made a similar ware. Closer perhaps to crushed up and reformed glass, mixed with white clay, than to the harder, whiter Chinese porcelain, the French material is what we know as artificial or 'soft paste' porcelain, generally fired at a lower temperature than the 'hard

ABOVE *A Chinese porcelain coffee cup painted with a fable subject by Jeffrey Hamett O'Neale, purely English decoration enamelled in London; 6.5 cm (2½ in), 1750-1755.*

LEFT *A Chinese teapot painted in England in bright turquoise-green, the milestone in the foreground inscribed '57 miles to London'; 16 cm (6¼ in), c.1755.*

LEFT *An example of the earliest successful European porcelain, a blue and white candlestick made in France at St Cloud; 6 cm (2¼ in) late-seventeenth century.*

paste' porcelain of China. St. Cloud is creamy in colour and surprisingly thick and heavy – unlike the Chinese – but it could be painted in blue beneath the glaze in the same way as the oriental porcelain, and, above all, was highly translucent. This was the only European porcelain for about twenty years until Johann Friedrich Böttger, an alchemist working for Augustus, King of Saxony, perfected in his castle laboratories a realistic copy of Chinese hard paste. In around 1710 the first Böttger porcelain was made, and subsequent improvements meant that by the 1720s the Meissen factory was producing a pure, hard white porcelain which, if anything, was whiter and smoother than most Chinese. Whether left plain white or enamelled in oriental or German styles, Meissen is distinguished by the quality of the porcelain body.

With its closely guarded secret recipe, the Meissen factory, under the patronage of Augustus, had a virtual monopoly in Europe until the secrets leaked out. At the Du Paquier factory in Vienna, and subsequently at Berlin and elsewhere, similar fine porcelain was made with kaolin mined in Germany. It could be enamelled in any style and, because it was in many ways superior to the Chinese, oriental decoration features less prominently in early German porcelain than more colourful and finely executed European styles. Figures, too, could be modelled in this brilliant white material and a new art form of ceramic sculpture in miniature was developed, led by the masterly work of J. J. Kaendler at Meissen.

Trade restrictions meant that, while quantities of Chinese

RIGHT *A Meissen large vase painted with so-called* indianesche Blumen, *an adaptation of an oriental style which was to have considerable influence on English porcelain, c. 1735.*

porcelain came into England for sale in the middle of the eighteenth century, no German porcelain was permitted to be sold in England. What little did arrive was by private trade, frequently given by the German court as diplomatic gifts to ambassadors or generals. Chinese porcelain remained the major influence on the English pottery industry of the day, with delftware and stoneware fighting to compete.

By the 1740s a method of making a fine white stoneware glazed with salt had been perfected in Staffordshire. Although technically pottery, when very thin it could sometimes be slightly translucent and, more importantly, it could withstand hot liquids fairly well. Copies of Chinese porcelain were produced in the thickly-glazed white saltglaze ware, although a certain English rustic charm and shapes based on English pewter gave the Staffordshire saltglazed

wares a very provincial and unsophisticated feel.

It was inevitable that sooner or later a method would be found to produce porcelain in England. The market was there; all that was needed was a suitable recipe and the skill to produce a translucent body commercially. Meissen, like many other continental factories, had unlimited financial backing from the Saxon court. In England there was no such royal patronage available and any porcelain factory had to raise its own finance to sustain itself while experiments perfected the porcelain body and kilns. This did not happen overnight, and the difficult first few years of the English porcelain industry are, in many people's view, the most interesting and exciting.

ABOVE *A group of French soft paste porcelain wares, the teapot St Cloud, the soup bowl and jar Mennecy; second quarter of eighteenth century. The creamy soft paste in contrast to harder white Chinese porcelain.*

Chapter Two
The First Ten Years

Collectors will always argue over which was the first English porcelain factory, but really there is only one which can begin to lay claim to the title. A Frenchman, Thomas Briand, brought the secret of porcelain making to London and addressed the Royal Society in 1742 or 1743, showing examples of porcelain which he claimed to have made. He entered into some sort of partnership with Nicholas Sprimont, a Huguenot silversmith living in exile in London, and Chelsea porcelain was born. Briand was the chemist and adventurer, Sprimont the artist and craftsman who understood London society. He frequented the coffee houses of the day where he conversed with artists such as William Hogarth. Taste in the London of the 1740s was breaking away rapidly from the formal baroque to the flowing shell forms of the rococo, and while Sprimont's silver reflected this taste, the whiteness and softness of porcelain seemed even more suitable for the exciting flower shapes inspired by nature. Shell-shaped salt containers surrounded by lobsters or crayfish, or coffee pots and beakers heavily modelled with flowers, leaves and gnarled twigs are found in English silver of the 1740s, the work of Paul de

BELOW *A Chelsea 'crayfish' salt based on a silver original by Nicholas Sprimont. Strong colours are contrasted with the whiteness of the porcelain; 12 cm (4½ in), c.1752.*

Lamerie being much more important than that of Sprimont. These silver vessels were the inspiration for wonderful shapes in early Chelsea porcelain, usually left in the white to emphasize the strong modelling — illustrated here. When coloured, the enamels were gaudy and bright, but were applied discriminatingly, always ensuring that plenty of white porcelain showed – the whiteness of which Sprimont could be justly proud. The best known shape, and most important to historians, is the so-called 'Goat and Bee' jug, curiously modelled after a silver idea with an applied honey bee by the lip. Many examples are known in glazed, creamy white porcelain and a few are incised with 'Chelsea 1745'. A single example is dated 1743, and if one believes this is the date of manufacture rather than the date it is commemorating, then this is the earliest known dated piece of English porcelain, providing a link with Briand's experimental porcelain shown to the Royal Society in 1742 or 1743.

The Goat and Bee jugs, made no later than 1745, show that in its infancy the Chelsea factory was able to produce a highly translucent white porcelain body, evenly fired and thinly cast with great delicacy. As a silversmith Sprimont probably understood the techniques of casting, using plaster moulds and liquid clay. Early Chelsea teawares thrown on a potter's wheel or pressed into hollow revolving plaster moulds are not nearly so finely made. Certainly cups and saucers made at Chelsea do not begin to compare with the thin Chinese teawares. To be successful, Sprimont had to make something nobody could buy in London, and here he was helped by trade restrictions preventing the public sale of any German porcelain in England. European designs, which took several years to order from distant Canton, could be painted at Chelsea in a matter of weeks. The artists at Chelsea copied Meissen porcelain borrowed from collectors, while at the same time they created a style of flower painting which was more splendid and freely painted than Meissen's *deutsche Blumen*. Chinese patterns played no part in the output of the Chelsea factory. Interestingly, the factory noted that collectors were very keen on the Japanese porcelain known as Kakiemon, imported into England at the beginning of the eighteenth century. Meissen had copied this twenty years earlier, and either from Japan or from Meissen came the inspiration for many direct Chelsea copies of the Kakiemon style of bold coloured enamels offsetting the fine white porcelain ground. The European painting style of birds, flowers, landscapes and fables and the sought-after Kakiemon patterns could only be bought in England at Chelsea. And it is clear that for a few years no other English factory could come close to matching the quality of the Chelsea wares.

The monopoly which the Chelsea factory held for English-made porcelain was to last only a very short time, for others were working on their own recipes for the production of an artificial soft paste porcelain. Thomas Briand left Chelsea after only a year or two and settled in Staffordshire, although his death in 1747 brought to an end his new venture before it had really begun. Other potters were experimenting, but here we enter an area about which surprisingly little is known.

The study of the earliest English porcelain involves a great deal

BELOW *A Chelsea beaker with 'teaplant' moulding, left undecorated to show the factory's pride in the whiteness of its porcelain; 7 cm (2¾ in), 1745-1748.*

ABOVE *Chelsea copies of Japanese Kakiemon designs, a style which became very popular during the 1750s.*

of detective work. Little snippets of information gathered from writings and newspapers, helped occasionally by archaeological excavations and a certain amount of luck, have pieced together only the basic outlines of the story. The names of some of the principal characters are known, as well as the sites of some of the factories. Less clear is exactly what porcelain was made where. Several mysterious groups of porcelain have been brought together by collectors, and attempts have been made to put names to these. Much of the important original research has been done by Dr Bernard Watney who was the first to identify correctly many small factories and their wares. Several different factories in Liverpool resulted in problems of identification; there have been further difficulties in discovering what precisely was being made at sites in Bristol, Limehouse and Newcastle-under-Lyme. Luck has played a major part in providing vital evidence towards solving these puzzles. Workmen digging up the road just across the street from Liverpool Museum found pottery fragments discarded by Samuel Gilbody's porcelain works, and, in the 1960s, redevelopment on the site of the Pomona public house in Newcastle-under-Lyme produced the remains of an experimental kiln load of blue and white porcelain, including a bowl dated March 1746. Sadly though, as yet no finished examples have been found to link up with these kiln failures, which suggests that this particular venture in Newcastle was never a success.

Certain facts, however, are without question and can be recorded. Some time between 1745 and 1747, or early 1748, at Duke

Shore in Limehouse, East London, Joseph Wilson and Company made blue and white teapots, sauceboats and pickle dishes, probably using a newly discovered secret recipe including 'soaprock', a steatite mined in Cornwall. The venture failed, probably because of the poor translucence and crude appearance of the finished wares. Joseph Wilson moved to Newcastle-under-Lyme, where William Steer had been making porcelain. The unsuccessful wares found at the Pomona site are likely to have been made by William Steer. Steer and Wilson were in partnership until about 1755 and they probably made a successful porcelain, albeit clumsy and not well glazed. The class of porcelain originally attributed to William Reid's pot works in Liverpool is now strongly believed to have been made by Steer and Wilson at Newcastle-under-Lyme, based on experiments at Limehouse. Pickle dishes and sauceboats are again the principal products and include many features linked to the decoration on earlier Staffordshire saltglaze.

Meanwhile, the other principal partner in the Limehouse venture moved in 1748 or 1749 to Bristol. There Benjamin Lund made porcelain very similar to Limehouse wares, although somewhat improved. We can be certain about some of the products of Lund's factory, for several sauceboats are marked with the name 'Bristol' embossed on the base, and a figure of a Chinaman is inscribed 'Bristol 1750'. A small cream jug which is typical of Lund's blue and white porcelain, is shown on page 20. This particular example, although thickly potted, is evenly glazed – a considerable

RIGHT *A Lund's Bristol cream jug, delightfully unsophisticated; 6.7 cm (2½ in), c.1750.*

ABOVE *A Vauxhall creamboat painted in blue, 14 cm (5½ in) long, c.1755. Misshapen and primitive, but this all adds to its charm.*

improvement on the wares believed to have been made at Limehouse. It was offered for sale in a provincial auction room in 1981 in a mixed lot catalogued as Chinese. A London dealer spotted it and, having bought it quite cheaply, brought it to my department at Phillips for confirmation of its early date. I instantly recognized what it was and could hardly contain my excitement, for it was the most attractive piece of Bristol I had seen in a long time. We sold it for £3,200, a high price then, but, looking back, it seems quite reasonable now. How can this simple cup be so valuable? I have studied the rare porcelain of this period and have developed an inherent love of blue and white. Perhaps it is just the rarity or the sense of achievement as Benjamin Lund struggles to improve the failed Limehouse porcelain into a successful commercial enterprise in Bristol. But, to me, this jug was as exciting as a newly discovered early work by a great painter would be to a picture specialist. It points the way to greater things, for, in 1751, Lund moved his business to Worcester, swallowed up by a major new partnership who were determined to make something more of this revolutionary china body.

In a space of seven years we have seen five different ventures struggling to make a success of a very similar formula. We will discover in the following chapters how this success was to be achieved at Worcester. In the meantime we are left with a large number of pieces of blue and white porcelain, some slotting easily into a particular place in this early history, others posing far too many problems to begin to answer, and all indicating just how much more there is still to be discovered about English porcelain of the mid-eighteenth century.

ABOVE *A range of Bow blue and white wares, the saucer of 1748-50 contrasted with two plates from the 1760s.*

In the autumn of 1988 the publication of a new report on an archaeological excavation meant that a whole class of porcelain had to be re-attributed. An extensive range of blue and white and coloured teawares and ornamental shapes had, prior to the new report, been classified, for want of a better name, as the work of the Liverpool potter and porcelain maker William Ball. The date seemed right, and certain features of this class corresponded to delft painting, Liverpool being a centre for delft manufacture. The group, however, did not fit happily into a Liverpool collection and many people looked for evidence to place the group elsewhere. The proof, leading to the publication of the report, came when unglazed fragments and kiln failures exactly matching this distinctive porcelain were found in London, on the site of a delft and stoneware pottery in Vauxhall. Records show that porcelain was made there during the 1750s and 1760s and all textbooks on the subject now need to be re-written. In addition, these discoveries mean that William Ball becomes just another name working in Liverpool, as we do not now know what he was making. 'William Ball' porcelain, now called Vauxhall, has many affinities to the other great London factory of Bow, and it is not too surprising that the two wares originate from the same city.

The factory on Stratford Road in Bow, in East London, began

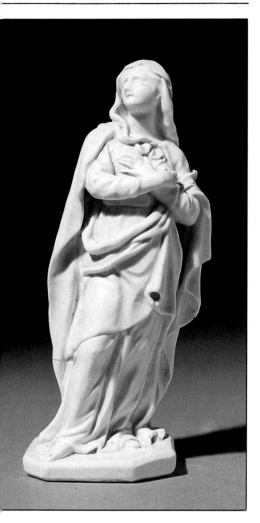

ABOVE *A figure of the Mater Dolorosa produced by the 'Girl in a Swing' factory after an ivory carving, the sculptural quality ideally suited to the soft porcelain; 19.5 cm (7½ in), c.1750. Sold in September 1985 for £5,300.*

by making crude and simple wares, although it was to become one of the largest producers of soft paste porcelain in England. The exact date of the factory's opening is unclear. However, the principal partners – Thomas Frye, a painter, and Edward Heylyn, a merchant and glassmaker – took out a patent as early as 1744 for making a material 'of the same nature or kind, and equal to, if not exceeding in goodness and beauty, China or Porcelain ware imported from abroad'. Production probably began fully in 1747, and certainly in 1748 when the factory was visited by Daniel Defoe it was described as a large manufactory which had 'already made large quantities of Teacups, etc . . . little inferior to those which are brought from China'.

The following year two new partners joined the Bow factory: John Weatherby and John Crowther, china and glass dealers who, it is known, had connections in Staffordshire with Thomas Briand, late of Chelsea. The enlarged premises at Bow were built as a copy of the warehouse of the East India Company at Canton in China. Indeed the factory styled itself 'New Canton', the name used on a small number of documentary inkwells dated 1750 and 1751.

The Bow factory was much more enterprising and, it would seem, more successful than Chelsea, for it grew to a remarkable size. Records show a massive turnover of £18,715 8s. 9d. in 1754, and from insurance details it was clearly the largest china factory in England. The products were not as restricted as other London enterprises, and while they seem to have made a small number of European styles, it was the Chinese influence which dominated the factory's wares for at least a decade. This was in complete contrast to the styles produced at Chelsea. Copies of Chinese *famille rose* designs appear initially on very English shapes such as shell salts and centrepieces, sauceboats and mugs with spreading bases; these were shapes hard to obtain from dealers in Chinese porcelain. Coloured tewares from the early years at Bow are surprisingly uncommon, which, again, reveals that the factory was aiming to produce products that would fill gaps in the market. Probably because it was less expensive, much of Bow was sold in white with only moulded decoration, copying the Chinese, while the bulk of the production was in underglaze blue, always directly reproducing popular oriental originals.

Before discussing some of these wares in greater detail, mention should be made of two other early porcelain makers in London, both of whom remain very much shrouded in mystery. The work of one consists of the so-called 'A'-marked wares, a class of enamelled porcelain sometimes bearing the letter A in enamel underneath, as a form of mark. Dating from the 1740s, some of the decoration is copied from contemporary engravings published in London, and the general theme links up with rococo styles much used in England at that time. Production must have been very limited, as only a very small number of examples survive. The white porcelain figure of a girl in a swing gives the name to an extensive range of porcelain at one time thought to be Chelsea, but probably made elsewhere in London in the early 1750s. The distinctive modelling of the girl is seen on a wide range of so-called 'toys' – scent bottles, needle cases, and seals formed as

figures, animals and natural shapes. Many similar novelties or toys were made at Chelsea and it is often very difficult to tell the two apart, except by the facial characteristics of the female characters depicted. The 'Girl in a Swing' factory made a very small number of tearwares in addition to some ambitious figure groups, and the white sculpture of the Mater Dolorosa, illustrated opposite, shows that at its best this factory's production was in no way inferior to Chelsea, although it has a more provincial feel to it. Some people believe this class was made in a separate department within the Chelsea factory, while others regard it as being a totally separate establishment in London, probably connected with a jeweller and merchant named Guyat. The mystery of where it was made has conjured up much speculation; even a romantic novel by Richard Adams is based on the chance discovery of a coloured 'Girl in a Swing'. Hopefully, however, new evidence will be found soon to end any speculation about the two different Chelsea factories.

Our knowledge of the first ten years of English porcelain has advanced significantly since the first research by the English Porcelain Circle in the 1920s. Yet, as I have shown in this chapter, there is still a great deal of scope for research; this is an area where it is possible for anyone to find that 'missing link' with a little patience, dedication, and luck. Undoubtedly, over the next decade many new and important discoveries will be made.

ABOVE *Two scent bottles from the 'Girl in a Swing' factory, with characteristic modelling, 1750-1753. Only 7 cm (2¾ in) high, these 'toys' have obvious appeal.*

BELOW *A Bow butter tub painted in Japanese style but with the design treated in an English fashion; 12.5 cm (5 in) wide, c.1752.*

Chapter Three
The Oriental Connection

ABOVE *Even a photograph conveys the delicate thinness of this early Worcester coffee cup of 1752-1753, 6 cm (2¼ in) high. It sold in June 1988 for £2,960, in spite of a tiny chip.*

During its infancy English-made porcelain was treated with suspicion. The public had become accustomed to eating off Chinese porcelain, and there is little doubt that the makers in England intended from the outset to pass their wares off as products of the Orient. In Chapter 2 I mentioned that the bulk of the Bow factory's wares were direct copies of Chinese, and the partners called their factory 'New Canton' further to imply a Chinese origin to their porcelain. The year after Bow coined the phrase, another factory began trading in a similar vein. In 1751 the 'Worcester Tonquin Manufactory' was established by a group of fifteen businessmen in Worcester, the most important partners being a local surgeon and amateur painter, Dr John Wall, and an apothecary, William Davis. Wall and Davis claimed to have invented a new formula for making porcelain and including a secret ingredient known only to them. In reality they had acquired their knowledge from the failing Bristol factory, which was transferred up the River Severn to newly built premises at Worcester. Benjamin Lund, the proprietor at Bristol who had learnt his trade at Limehouse, is recorded as living in Worcester in 1752, and clearly he introduced the technology and probably supervised the building of the new kilns at the Worcester factory. By 1752 the works had overcome any teething problems and showed that, by altering the firing methods, the soaprock formula used at Bristol could be well controlled and, ultimately, perfected.

The thinly cast coffee cup illustrated here, and teapot on page 27 show that by about 1753 the Worcester factory was producing a delicate and finely moulded product capable of taking an even glaze. Slightly creamy in appearance, the quality of potting of these early wares is much higher than that of Bow or Chelsea, and they had one very significant advantage over their rivals. The presence of soaprock in the Worcester formula made the wares incredibly durable. They could sustain use with boiling water without cracking, a serious problem faced by most other manufacturers, particularly Chelsea and the products from the newly established factory at Derby. If you made tea in a Derby teapot in the 1750s the chances were it would crack open in front of you, all over your new Chippendale table! The calcined bone contained in Bow's secret recipe did not prevent this, but Worcester's bodies were remarkably resilient to such treatment and gave Worcester a virtual monopoly on the making of fine, long-lasting tea services. For this reason they concentrated on producing tea and coffee wares to the almost complete exclusion of all other shapes. Vast quantities of teapots and cups and saucers were made, and many survive today. Indeed, a survey of all eighteenth-century porcelain sold at Phillips in any one year will show that far more Worcester wares survive than wares from almost all of the other

factories put together. Worcester teapots are fairly common, whilst Bow teapots are very hard to find and Chelsea and Derby ones virtually non-existent. We will see in the next chapter that Bow and Derby turned to figure making to compensate for the loss of the teaware trade to Worcester; this accounts for the scarcity.

Perhaps it was with an air of confidence that Worcester was able to put its goods on the market with a unique style of painting, only lightly based on the Chinese. Bow, you will remember, used Chinese prototypes for virtually all of its early wares, particularly the blue and white. On the other hand, direct copies of Chinese in early Worcester are surprisingly rare. Worcester's skill lay in adapting the patterns which came over from China into a style of its own, more suited to the English public. They took Chinese *famille rose* designs and combined them with a style of formal painting and palette borrowed heavily from the *indianesche Blumen* style used at Meissen. The result was a decoration which appeared Chinese, but would actually have been quite alien to a Chinese artist. The painters at Worcester presented to their customers not authentic Chinese patterns but rather their own vision of the Orient. In their factory workshops, looking at Chinese porcelain, they had no concept of what the designs represented. They could not begin to understand what life was like in the Far East. Any ideas they did have would have come from prints published in England and accounts of travellers, merchants and missionaries from the days of Marco Polo onwards.

ABOVE *Although missing the finials, this garniture is the finest example of early Worcester ever to pass through Phillips' rooms. Made c.1753, they represent pure chinoiserie as only Worcester knew how to make it.*

RIGHT *A Lowestoft mug directly copying a commercial Chinese export tankard of c.1770 and having more charm and life than the original; 9 cm (3½ in).*

But even these did not present a very authentic picture, because the Chinese jealously guarded their culture and allowed the foreigners very little access to their people. Fact was thus often clouded by fiction. The dealers in England selling Chinese wares added to the confusion by deliberately promoting the fantastic elements of the oriental image, to give their goods a more mystical air. In the English adaptations of oriental designs we find incredible bubble-headed people, in a land of peculiar bridges, crazy rocks and strange pagoda-like buildings which could never stand. Everything was out of proportion. Animals were too small or too big and figures sometimes dwarfed their houses and pagodas. This is chinoiserie.

The garniture of vases shown on page 25 had always been passed down as Chinese, but they were brought into me because their owner felt that the Chinamen seemed to have an English accent. His suspicion was correct, for these pieces were actually made at Worcester in the early 1750s, and it is unlikely that the artist had ever seen a real Chinaman. His figures were probably more akin to the characters he saw in Worcester High Street, suitably adapted to look oriental. His landscapes were certainly not based on Worcestershire, but neither were they Chinese. They fall somewhere in between,

LEFT *An exciting rococo shape inspired by English silver contrasting the simple Chinese 'Staghunt' pattern used on this Worcester teapot of c.1753, 13 cm (5 in) high, this example sold in September 1988 for £7,320.*

conjured up out of a fantasy world in his mind.

Landscapes are often significant in identifying the maker of a piece of English porcelain, for each factory seemed to develop its own house style. Once you have seen a few Worcester landscapes, they become unmistakable. There is a certain way of painting rocks and trees, passed on from one painter to another and found on almost every example of the factory's oriental-style wares. Painters in Liverpool followed very similar styles, but tended towards looser, less detailed designs, with heavy reliance on dots as a feature. Lowestoft's ideas of Chinese landscapes have such a childlike quality about them that they could not have been painted anywhere else. It takes quite a while to learn these major differences between the factories, but it is worth pursuing, as it is often easier to distinguish a factory by its painting than its body, glaze, or shapes.

It is difficult to see why the English decorators went to the trouble of creating these different styles and designs if the intention was purely to imitate the Chinese. They could all have copied the Chinese originals with far less effort involved. Early Bow porcelain was probably produced in an attempt to compete directly with the Chinese by providing wares which looked very much like Chinese pots, but were far cheaper. The idea at Worcester was, I feel, to try to improve upon the Chinese by making the designs more 'English', hence appealing to the taste of the English public. Their porcelain must have been more expensive than the oriental wares, and yet it sold well. Perhaps, too, this was because the Worcester wares were decorative and, much more importantly, were fun, in a way that the Chinese pots were not. China and the Orient were alien to most people. Worcester's designs reflected much more what everyone thought the Orient ought to look like, and the shapes were often more familiar to the home market. This is revealed in the teapot illustrated

RIGHT *A Chelsea beaker and two small vases from the Bow factory, all c.1753 and exactly copying Japanese designs popular fifty years earlier.*

on page 27. The pattern, a direct copy of the Chinese, is known as 'The Staghunt' and was used widely at Worcester and at Liverpool. On plain shapes it could be mistaken for Chinese, but such an eccentric rococo style could only have been made in England. It has the same feel as George II silver and English carved furniture of the period, trying so hard to be a fine piece but looking slightly incongruous. A Chinese staghunt really is out of place on so European a shape. Chelsea knew this and did not mimic the Chinese styles. Bow was careful to produce faithful copies of Chinese shapes as well as designs. Worcester, however, happily intermingled Chinese styles with European and were remarkably successful in creating their own niche in the market for English porcelain.

By the mid 1750s the English public were presented with a vast choice in porcelain. All of the factories experimented with designs until they found their own particular style, and a healthy competition developed in the London trade. Those firms whose quality slipped and who failed to read the fashions correctly did not survive. So, a new twist to the imitation business developed. Factories ended up not only copying exactly from the Chinese and European styles, but also from each other. Bow and Lowestoft copied Worcester, Worcester borrowed from Bow, and everyone copied Chelsea. After a while certain designs became universal, each factory producing virtually the same version of a popular pattern. For identification purposes this creates great confusion.

Perhaps the wares most difficult to distinguish are the direct copies of oriental porcelain. Most factories advertised that they could make replacements for pieces of foreign china which had been broken. Worcester, for instance, claimed that its enamelled wares so closely resembled the finest foreign china that it made up pieces for costly, broken sets without any perceptible difference. Plenty of

LEFT *The 'Lady in a Pavilion' pattern copied by Chelsea directly from a Japanese Kakiemon original; Raised Anchor period, c.1750.*

examples survive to show that such a claim was not simply salesmanship. Kakiemon porcelain from Japan, unobtainable in England in the mid-eighteenth century, was copied by every factory, but particularly at Chelsea and Bow. The English porcelain was soft paste and had a very different feel. This is especially true in the case of Chelsea. But, from a photograph alone it is usually quite impossible to tell whether a teabowl and saucer is genuine Japanese or a copy made in London. The customers probably did not care.

By 1760, English porcelain was so well established that the copying of designs began to work in reverse. Instead of simply sending silver prototypes for the Chinese to copy, East Indiamen took private cargoes of English china to be reproduced exactly, shipped back to England and still be sold in London at a cheaper price than the original. These copies were in hard paste porcelain and, of course, the Chinese painters had the same problems in interpreting the English designs as the English did in interpreting their ideas; despite this fact, the provenance of some pieces can be very confusing. Recently, I argued with the oriental porcelain specialists at Phillips over an item which was included in a sale of Chinese porcelain. I demanded to know why a Derby basket had been included in their sale rather than be passed on to my English ceramics department. They could not understand what I meant, and it was only when I took the piece out of the cabinet that I realized that it was indeed Chinese. Dating from about 1765, a characteristic Derby basket had been copied exactly. The bird painting was in bright enamel colours and the modelling of the flowerheads in the intersections of the arcaded sides was faithfully reproduced. The Chinese, in particular, made copies of Worcester blue and white dishes and sauceboats, but I have also seen Chinese versions of Bow and Liverpool porcelain. They tend to be rare, and this could make a fascinating area to collect, especially as the copies usually fetch less than the English originals.

Chapter Four
The Influence of Meissen and English Figure Making

While the Chinese trade was the most important influence on early English porcelain, there were a significant number of wealthy customers who wanted something different. Meissen porcelain, or 'Dresden' as it was generally known, had prior to the mid-eighteenth century been available in only small quantities. There was little direct trade with Germany and the pieces owned by the English gentry were frequently gifts, such as snuff boxes, delicate tea services, and figurines.

At Chelsea, the proprietor Nicholas Sprimont was very interested in these wares and felt that there would be a ready market in London for the much more European styles. It is known that, at every opportunity, Sprimont borrowed examples of Meissen porcelain for his painters to copy – although very little seems to have been available before 1750. Until that time English silver, via Sprimont's direct influence, inspired most of the factory's products. The change in direction of the Chelsea factory occurred during the 'Raised Anchor' period, in around 1750-1752. Three styles of painting, previously unknown except on the precious Dresden wares, became available to the English public. The first, the Kakiemon style, has been discussed in the previous chapter, although it is worth repeating that the designs were much more likely to have been copied from Meissen's own imitations, rather than from the Japanese originals. Flowers and landscapes constitute the other major themes which Chelsea set out to copy.

It is unnecessary to recount here a full history of painting at Meissen, except to mention a few important names. The most famous painter, J. G. Heroldt, was the master of the chinoiserie, although by 1750 this style was old fashioned and no direct English copies have come to light. European landscapes were painted by many artists, in particular by C. F. Herold and G. B. Hauer. Middle Eastern merchants in harbour scenes and rural landscapes featuring expanses of water gave an excuse to leave large areas of porcelain exposed, the whiteness of which Meissen was justly proud. Flower bouquets, sprigs and fanciful insects were a speciality of Meissen, where they were referred to as *deutsche Blumen*. One painter, Johann Gottfried Klinger, developed a method of painting insects and flowers which cast a shadow on the porcelain. This so-called *ombrierte* style of painting gave a particularly three-dimensional effect.

At Chelsea, the flower painting was copied exactly, with some pieces including shadows. The plate shown opposite, from the 'Red Anchor' period, is in shape and pattern almost indistinguishable

from Meissen, even to the extent that the rim is edged with a fine brown line. No deceit was intended, however, for the plate is clearly marked with a tiny anchor in red, the sign to the English public that they were buying Chelsea porcelain.

The identity of the landscape painters at Chelsea has been debated by collectors for more than a century. The principal contenders were William Duvivier and a Frenchman named Lefevre, alongside the best known of all, Jeffrey Hamett O'Neale. Duvivier specialized in Meissen-style landscapes, including merchants with barrels in harbour scenes, after C. F. Herold. He seems to have favoured painting in a purple-pink monochrome, a style much used in Europe. O'Neale's name is synonymous with subjects from fables, colourful landscapes with animals representing the tales of Aesop

ABOVE *Directly copying Meissen, a Chelsea plate in which the white porcelain is used to excellent effect; 23.5 cm (9¼ in), red anchor mark, c.1755.*

and Lafontaine. He started painting in London on white Chinese porcelain, and a Chinese coffee cup with one of his distinctive fables is illustrated on page 12. He joined Chelsea in around 1753 and subsequently moved to Worcester.

Because of their rarity and considerable charm, the early Chelsea landscape wares are very sought-after by collectors and are, therefore, expensive. The earliest flower painting is also costly, but simple flowers on plates and dishes of the later 1750s can be surprisingly inexpensive. The plate shown on page 31 was one of a pair sold at Phillips in 1989. The lovely smooth white feel of the Chelsea glaze is finely represented by these plates.

The styles of decoration that originated at Chelsea very soon spread to other factories. Bow remained dominated by the Chinese style, but by the late 1750s some European flower painting was being tried, although of an inferior quality to Chelsea. A little earlier, Meissen-style painting was introduced at Worcester. Their speciality was fine, large jugs with extensive landscapes, often bearing armorial panels. Their scenes of ruins in landscapes, painted in purple monochrome, can also be particularly fine. On a simpler scale, birds in trees and spreading flower sprays were painted on dishes and vases, some by the artist James Rogers who used a particularly rich palette featuring a flame-orange enamel.

Worcester's flower painting is rather more formal than the meticulous realism of Meissen and Chelsea. The garniture of vases illustrated here are of various oriental-style shapes which had become standard forms at Meissen and were well-suited to mantelpieces in the elegant homes in London. The painting is much freer than that of Chelsea, and in many ways is much more suited to

LEFT *A Worcester beer jug painted by James Rogers in about 1757, an imposing shape with wonderfully rich decoration; 20 cm (8 in).*

BELOW *Inspired by Meissen, these Worcester vases have been adapted to the softer colouring and painting style popular in the late 1750s. The dramatic shapes and decoration work very well together. 21.5 cm (8½ in) high.*

ABOVE *A Derby dish of lively rococo shape with the appealing charm associated with the so-called 'moth painter', c.1765.*

the creamy blue tint of the Worcester porcelain. It is some way removed from true Meissen, but, even so, the Meissen mark of the crossed swords was occasionally added to products at the Worcester factory.

Two other factories were strongly influenced by Meissen in the 1750s. At Derby, it seems that there was less variety in painted decoration, though their own style of strongly coloured and finely drawn flower painting was developed. Certain fruits, in particular cherries, are often included in the Derby flower groupings. The factory's porcelain body was inferior to Worcester's and consequently examples are much rarer, although not necessarily more valuable. The Staffordshire porcelain factory established by William Littler at Longton Hall had considerable trouble with its porcelain, and examples from the first few years after 1750 can be very crude in comparison with their competitors. By the mid-1750s, however, their paste was much improved and they began production of a wide range of exciting shapes, characterized by a rustic quality unique to Longton Hall.

Vessels in the shape of vegetable forms and animals had been made in China and at Meissen, although some of the most fabulous examples came from the German and French tin-glazed earthenware factories. In England, it was Chelsea and Longton Hall who dominated this market. From Staffordshire came tureens in the shape

ABOVE *A Longton Hall sauceboat, the leaf moulding so characteristic that it could not have been made by any other factory. 14.5 cm (5¾ in), c.1755.*

of melons or birds, and all manner of shapes formed from overlapping leaves. Strongly veined in puce, and edged in bright green and yellow, these wares became a hallmark of the Longton Hall factory, and remain remarkably sought-after today. Plates and dishes with moulded borders of strawberry leaves were the most popular, the centres painted with birds or flowers in similar-strong colours, and even more stylized than those of Worcester. Sprays of roses and other flowers among wispy leaves and fine tendrils are said to be the work of an unknown 'Trembly Rose' painter, although probably several men were responsible for this distinctive style.

Chelsea tureens are undoubtedly some of the most remarkable objects ever made in English porcelain. Large vessels with separate covers and stands were made in shapes ranging from cauliflowers and bundles of asparagus to really splendid animals. A large rabbit, a pair of fighting cockerels, a giant eel and a swan are among the fabulous creations; probably the most incredible large tureen is shaped as a boar's head resting on a dish complete with vegetable garnishes and a serving knife with a porcelain handle lying alongside. Naturally very rare, an example was sold at auction in 1974 for £30,000, and would be worth a great deal more than that today. It may not be to everyone's taste, but you cannot fail to admire the skill of the craftsmen who thought up such creations in about 1755.

RIGHT *The provincial charm of Longton Hall seen on a strawberry plate of 1755-1758. The bird painting should be compared with the more exciting Worcester jug of roughly similar date. (page 32). 23.5 cm (9¼ in).*

BELOW *A Chelsea tureen and cover in the form of a bundle of asparagus. The factory made many exciting tureen shapes which livened up a dinner table, the shape reflected the intended contents; 17.5 cm (7 in) long. Red anchor marks, c.1755.*

Another revolutionary style introduced at Chelsea at the same time was a purely English invention, using the Meissen *deutsche Blumen* sprays and combining them with single large botanical specimens. The so-called 'Hans Sloane' wares were faithfully copied from prints by famous botanists such as Philip Miller, who published drawings of the Physic Garden in Chelsea. Sir Hans Sloane, a patron of the Chelsea porcelain factory, provided actual specimens of plants and rare butterflies for the painters to copy. In the richness of thick ceramic colours, the plants remain as fresh today as when they were painted and, although collections of such pieces are rare today, grouped together as they are on page 39, these pieces make a truly wonderful display. This collection sold at Phillips in March 1989 for between £530 for single chipped plates and £16,500 each for the large oval dishes.

You can imagine how a table set out with a whole botanical service must have looked in the eighteenth century, and how proud the original owners must have been. Decorating a table for dinner, or more especially for dessert became very important in the 1750s. Improvements in road transportation meant that it was easier to invite guests to visit a country house and, at the same time, the host wanted to impress his wealth upon his visitors.

Table decorations first became popular in the seventeenth century when figures were modelled out of sugar and coloured icing and placed among the guests at a banquet, along with towers of shimmering jellies and other confectionery. In Germany, by the 1740s, Meissen china figures had replaced the sugar creations, and some of them eventually found their way to England. In 1753, Horace Walpole wrote how the '. . . jellies, biscuits, sugar plumbs and creams have long given way to harlequins, gondoliers, Turks, Chinese and shepherdesses of Saxon China.' It became popular for certain of the nobility in England to collect Meissen figures not only for display during dessert, but also as ornaments for cabinets and to be displayed in compartments in rococo furniture. In 1751, Sir Charles Hanbury Williams lent his collection of Meissen to Sir Edward Fawkener, an important patron of the Chelsea factory, so that the figures and wares could be copied exactly by the artists at the factory. Prior to the Meissen influence, figures at Chelsea had been primitive affairs, restricted to a few white Chinamen and goddesses. The exception seems to have been a fine sculpture of 'Trump', the pug dog which was as well known in London artistic society as its owner, William Hogarth. Trump had been modelled in terracotta by the distinguished sculptor Roubiliac, and Nicholas Sprimont, who was probably acquainted with both Hogarth and Roubiliac, obtained a cast or mould. Three copies are known in Chelsea porcelain, made prior to 1750. One of these, a coloured example from the Rous Lench collection holds the record price for any English porcelain. It was sold in 1985 by Sotheby's for £85,800.

During the Red Anchor period, Chelsea made many figures either directly copied from or closely inspired by Meissen originals. J. J. Kaendler, the genius responsible for most figures made at Meissen, used the porcelain to a most successful effect. Colouring was restricted to strongly coloured areas and features, but various parts were left plain white. This heavily contrasted method was used to similar effect at Chelsea, particularly in the early 1750s, although later on they tended rather to overdo the colouring. Late in the 1750s, Joseph Willems became the factory's principal modeller and, although drawing heavily from Meissen, he frequently added his own distinctive characteristics to the modelling. The young boys struggling with a fish, illustrated here, are remarkably sculptural, the flesh tones only lightly painted to emphasize the quality of the model.

RIGHT *Modelled by Joseph Willems, this Chelsea group is delicately coloured in the manner of Meissen; 22 cm (8½ in), c.1758.*

FAR RIGHT *Botanical decoration, known as 'Hans Sloane', is probably the best known of all Chelsea porcelain. This fine collection was sold at Phillips in 1988. The large dishes, 7 cm (14½ in) wide, were made c.1755.*

In around 1750-1752, the Bow factory was producing two very different sorts of figures. Some were modelled directly after Meissen, although not nearly of the same quality as Chelsea. The other sort were all modelled by one person, whose name is not known, but whose work is extraordinarily distinctive. Just as the 'Girl in a Swing' models can be recognized by facial features (see Chapter 2), the works of the 'Muses' modeller are quite unmistakable. Whether he was modelling a Greek goddess, a Chinese figure, or an old woman, the faces on his models are the same, typified by the figure illustrated opposite. The name by which he is known derives from a set of single figures of the Greek Muses which he modelled. However, he is better known for two major groups in his amusing rustic style – 'The Fortune Teller, and 'The Goddess Ki Ma Sao and her Attendants'. The latter, modelled after a painting by Watteau, is more at home amongst a collection of early English pottery figures than amongst fine porcelain, but the work of the 'Muses' modeller is still fun, more fun really than the rather better made Bow figures of the later 1750s and 1760s.

While modelling improved, the decoration of Bow figures changed for the worse. Particularly strong opaque enamel colours were used all over the figures and were applied much more heavily than the refined colouring seen on Chelsea figures of the same period. The bases, originally plain mounds, became more and more ornamented with scrollwork, a trend we will be looking at in Chapter 6. In the meantime, there is a third major figuremaker to consider, namely Derby.

At Derby, Meissen again had an influence, but much less directly than at Chelsea. New figures were inspired by Meissen, but included elements characteristic of Derby. The works at Derby had been established in about 1748 by Andrew Planche, a Huguenot who came originally from London where it is likely that he had connections with the Chelsea works. It has been suggested that he acquired the secret of making porcelain from either Thomas Briand or Nicholas Sprimont (see Chapter 1). It was during this early period, from 1750 to 1755, that some of the finest figures were made at Derby. Known as 'dry edge', because of the absence of glaze underneath and around the edges of the bases, the simple models representing the seasons, the senses, rustic lovers, and Chinamen, are coloured in a delightful soft palette, relying on delicate colours to contrast with the white porcelain. The seated shepherdess holding a model of a Derby porcelain basket, is one of my favourites (see back cover illustration). Generally speaking, Derby figures are inexpensive considering their quality and beauty. After 1756, when Planche was joined at Derby by the porcelain enameller William Duesbury, the colouring and modelling of figures became more elaborate, as befitted the taste of the day. In terms of colouring and the crispness of the modelling, Derby figures are far superior to those made at Bow, their principal rival. The wide scroll bases are strongly modelled, but picked out in delicate greens and pale puce rather than the strong puce and blue used at Bow. By the mid-1760s the output of figures at these two factories was very considerable indeed.

ABOVE *A Worcester figure by John Toulouse, c.1765, far inferior to Bow or Derby of the same period, but with a naive charm; 15.5 cm (6 in).*

RIGHT *A Bow figure of 'Hope' in the distinctive style of the 'Muses Modeller', c.1755, 21.5cm (8½ in).*

Longton Hall should be mentioned here as a further major figuremaker, producing pieces similar in style and taste to those of Derby. Problems with firing, as well as finance, meant that the output of figures from Longton Hall was much smaller and, consequently, examples tend to be rare and expensive. Early Longton Hall figures, from around 1750-1752, are of a type known as 'Snowman' because of the thick opaque white glaze with which they were covered. These figures are academic curios rather than things of beauty; nonetheless, they have become very rare and valuable today.

I mentioned previously the advantage Worcester had over its rivals as far as producing durable teawares. Derby, Bow, and Longton Hall all had inferior bodies and simply could not compete. However, in the area of figure making they were able to surpass Worcester. Indeed, Worcester neglected figure making – only a single Worcester figure model is known before 1760, and it is a feeble one at that. In about 1768, John Toulouse, a modeller from Bow, spent a short time at Worcester modelling only three pairs of figures and one single bird group before moving to Bristol. None of these are a credit to the factory, and it is no great loss that Worcester figures are so rare. Worcester's skill lay in the high quality teawares, and the factory confined itself to the area it knew best. Ironically, because Worcester figures are so rare, collectors will pay anything up to fifteen times as much as for the equivalent figures in Bow or Derby, even though in this case Derby would be of much better quality.

Eighteenth-century English figures are far more plentiful than Meissen and can make a very decorative collection. They look well when grouped together — opposite illustration — and it is not of great importance if they are damaged. Obviously damage will affect the value of a figure, but not to the same extent as, for example, a crack or a chip will affect a Chelsea plate. Chips to fingers, costume, or bases do not matter a great deal, as they are almost to be expected. When a neck has been broken it is altogether more serious and a model should be priced accordingly. I feel that figures are the area offering perhaps the greatest scope for a collector wishing to begin buying eighteenth-century English porcelain, as prices can be inexpensive.

RIGHT *A range of eighteenth-century English figures which convey a wonderful decorative effect. With some damage a collection like this need not be expensive:* Top Row – *Bow, Derby, Bow;* Second Row – *Bow;* Third Row – *Derby, Bow, Derby;* Bottom Row – *Chelsea, except for central piper, which is Derby.*

Chapter Five
Blue and White Porcelain

ABOVE *Sauceboats were an important product of all the early factories. These Worcester examples combine English silver shapes with Chinese decoration, c.1757.*

There is a simple reason why so much blue and white porcelain was made. Blue was the only colour which could be successfully fired at the same time as the glaze, and therefore the cost of manufacture was very much less than for coloured wares. The technology is simple to explain – the blue colour is an oxide of the rare metal cobalt. The Chinese discovered that once porcelain clay was completely dry, a vessel could be painted with this oxide mixed with water or oil. It was then coated with glaze which, chemically, differed very little from crushed glass mixed with water to make it sticky. In the heat of the kiln, this glaze melted, flowing evenly over the surface of the pot and then forming a single layer of crystalline glass as the kiln cooled down. The black cobalt oxide reacted chemically with the silicon in the glaze to form cobalt silicate, which is blue. Moreover, the blue colouring was chemically sealed within the surface glaze and could never fade or rub off, however much a vessel was used.

English blue and white is very similar, except that in most cases the formed clay pot was fired first before painting or glazing. This once-fired, unglazed material is known as 'biscuit', because it feels dry and rough to the touch. It was much easier to paint in cobalt oxide onto this fired biscuit china, and if it was then fired once again before glazing, the paint was hardened on and was less likely to run or blur in the kiln. If a piece required any colours other than blue, they had to be painted on top of the glaze and fired at a range of different temperatures, adding each time to the cost of the finished product. The 'underglaze blue' decoration, as it is known to collectors, is much more durable and would not be affected during use in the same way as some enamelled pieces. Little wonder, then, that the blue and white porcelain from China and subsequently English blue and white, was, and is, so popular.

Perhaps because it was relatively inexpensive, blue and white appealed more to the middle classes in England than to the nobility. For this reason, Chelsea blue and white is extremely rare. Nicholas Sprimont aimed for a more discerning, wealthy market, and did not consider it necessary to compete in London with Limehouse, Bow, and Vauxhall. Apart from very few cups and saucers, the only Chelsea blue and white normally encountered is a set of plates painted with a bird on a rock in the Chinese manner. One of the very few Chinese designs made at Chelsea, such a plate would fetch a high figure if offered for sale today. It is understandable that Chelsea did not want to try to compete with cheap imported Chinese services, but it is a pity that so few of these plates were made as technically and artistically they are superb.

The origins of English blue and white are discussed in Chapters 2 and 3. By the mid-1750s, various smaller makers had fallen by the wayside, leaving the market dominated by just two names – Worcester and Bow. Some small measure of success was achieved at Liverpool and Derby, while later on the stage was joined by the Lowestoft, Plymouth and Caughley works. Here, however, I mainly wish to tell the story of blue and white by looking at the wares of the greatest of all these makers, the Worcester china factory.

Although not necessarily well represented in public collections, the bulk of Worcester's output was decorated in underglaze blue. The factory saw this as its 'bread and butter' and it was sold in quantity to the middle classes, enabling the factory to produce its richer, more expensive coloured wares for the aristocracy. Bow had a similarly vast output of blue and white wares, but with its softer porcelain body the survival rate was much reduced compared with Worcester's durable soaprock body.

The public expected blue and white porcelain to come from China, and were not prepared to buy unless it looked Chinese. The first five or six years of the Worcester factory saw a growing sense of achievement as the factory perfected its blue and white wares. The primitive, naive designs of 1752-1753 developed gradually into very sophisticated patterns by 1757, changing significantly in style and quality. The factory would have been proud of this progression, but connoisseurs today tend to forget this as they lament the loss of the spontaneity of the earlier wares. The sauceboats illustrated opposite, dating from c.1757-1758, are clearly a considerable improvement on the primitive jug painted seven years earlier shown on page 20. I admire them both for very different reasons, but have to admit that I

ABOVE *A Worcester teapot painted with the 'Gazebo' pattern in Chinese style, a perfectly balanced design representing the best period of Worcester blue and white; 13cm (5 in), workman's mark, c.1756.*

would far rather own the simple Lund's Bristol jug than the superb Worcester sauceboats.

The factory, however, had reached the pinnacle of its success. The superb potting and perfection in design, represented by the 'Gazebo' pattern teapot shown here, display the qualities which place the factory far ahead of its rivals. This teapot, in perfect condition, was made before 1760 while the quality was at its best. The other teapot illustrated on page 49 was made *circa* 1770 and, while it is still a finely made piece, the execution and design do not match the example of fifteen years earlier.

By 1760, output was vast and every piece of blue and white had life and a refreshing handmade quality about it. The public bought as much as the factory was able to produce and so the proprietors looked for ways of increasing output whilst keeping costs low. They achieved this in two ways. First, they adapted the patterns so that they took less time to paint. Less finely detailed decoration and larger areas of plain shading could be added more quickly by less skilful painters. At the same time the use of the printing press revolutionized the ceramic industry, and in particular the manufacture of blue and white porcelain services.

Overglaze printing in enamel colours – principally black – had been perfected at Worcester by 1757. The two mugs with portraits of the King, illustrated here, show a degree of detail in the portraits that could not be produced by hand except by the very finest painters and at considerable cost. Underglaze printing was slower to develop but it was set to revolutionize the making of blue and white. Present day painters estimate that it would have taken something like half an hour to paint a typical saucer in the new formal styles. I have tried my hand at underglaze blue painting and, although by no means as accomplished as an eighteenth-century blue painter, I now realize

LEFT *Two fine Worcester mugs with overglaze transfer prints. These portraits of George II and George III are the first commercial Royal souvenirs made in English ceramics. 12 cm (4¾ in) and 14.5 cm, (5¾ in), 1758-1765.*

what an intricate job painting even a simple pattern must have been. Printing in underglaze blue was introduced in about 1756. By means of transferring the design from an engraved copper plate to the surface of the pot, an established pattern could be reproduced exactly in one fifteenth of the time it would have taken to paint.

A typical blue-printed teabowl and saucer is shown on page 48. The 'Fence' pattern was probably Worcester's best selling design, inspired by the Orient, but very much more English in its overall effect. The output of this pattern, and many others like it, reached staggering proportions; large quantities were exported to Holland where Chinese porcelain had previously found a major market. The success of Worcester was due mainly to their ability to match the Chinese exports in price. In June 1772 a Bath china shop advertised:

> 'Now on Sale . . . at Mainwarings, complete Tea Services of Blue and White Worcester China, from £1.15s. the set, consisting of 43 pieces . . .'

Six years later the same shop was selling Chinese tea services from £1.9s.; the price of Worcester was reasonably competitive. Earlier, in 1763, the *Oxford Journal* wrote strongly in favour of:

> '. . . the extraordinary strength and cheapness of the common sort of blue and white Worcester porcelain . . . an elegant desirable furniture calculated by its ease of purchase for general and ordinary use.'

The same journal warned, however, of imitations:

> 'The great abuse of it is the selling of other far inferior kinds of ware for Worcester, by which the buyer is deceived to his loss and the credit of the manufacture is injured.'

Worcester's success had indeed created a ready market for imitations. Other factories were now concentrating not so much on copying the Chinese, but instead on making careful imitations of most of Worcester's best selling shapes and patterns. The secret of Worcester's soaprock formula had already found its way to Liverpool, introduced there by Robert Podmore who had helped develop it at the Worcester works. Richard Chaffers had established a porcelain factory in Liverpool and in 1755 Podmore signed an agreement with him and Philip Christian to reveal the secret formula. By 1756 Chaffers and Christian were receiving their own supplies of soaprock from Cornwall. Chaffers died in 1765 and Philip Christian kept the

ABOVE *A selection of the many different Chinese designs used in Worcester blue and white, the central teapot of the 'Waiting Chinaman' pattern, c.1770, the other pieces at least ten years earlier.*

factory in production until 1776. Meanwhile, a new factory was established by Messrs. Pennington and Partners. It operated from about 1769 until 1799 and made similar but generally inferior wares.

Liverpool porcelain is easily confused with Worcester, especially when a very popular design such as the 'Cannonball' pattern was used at both factories. Chaffers' porcelain can have a blue-green tint, whereas the Christian body tends towards grey-green. Generally, Liverpool porcelain is much greener than that produced at Worcester. Certain styles of painting can also help distinguish Liverpool from Worcester, and another important clue is the shape of the foot-rims on cups and saucers. Worcester teawares usually have finely turned, even foot-rims, triangular in section and with the glaze wiped clear around the inside of the foot. Liverpool foot-rims tend to be undercut on the inside, producing an inward slanted section inside the base of the cup or bowl. While far from fool-proof, these differences are useful as a rough guide. Transfer printing in underglaze blue was not introduced at Liverpool until the Chaffers period in around 1770. Generally the quality was very poor and much inferior to Worcester. Some good quality overglaze black printing had been carried out earlier in Liverpool by Sadler and Green and others, but for some reason the secret techniques had not been perpetuated. By the time of the Pennington partnership, quality

RIGHT *An English version of a popular Chinese design known as the 'Jumping Boy', in this case on a small plate from Chaffers' factory in Liverpool; 12 cm (4¾ in), c.1758.*

of production had dropped dramatically and Liverpool was no match for Worcester.

A much more serious threat to Worcester's trade and reputation came from another factory, established in East Anglia in about 1757. The small port of Lowestoft seems an unlikely place to open a porcelain factory, but a local landowner's attempt to make use of the fine clay on his estate led to the setting up of a factory under the direction of Philip Walker and three partners. It is not thought that any significant production began before 1760, but by the following year evidence of dated pieces shows that the factory was producing a very white, somewhat chalky and not very translucent paste, decorated entirely in blue.

The wares produced at the Lowestoft factory always strike me as being very provincial. Initially Lowestoft did not try to copy Worcester directly, but concentrated on adapting the Chinese designs to their own style of painting. A freely painted cartoon-like style is much less precise than Worcester blue painting of the same

LEFT *A Lowestoft sweetmeat dish in the shape of a leaf, the naive painting typical of the early products of the Lowestoft factory; 14 cm (5½ in), painter no. 4, c.1760.*

date, and a great many wares seemed to have been aimed at the local market in the towns and villages of East Anglia. Lowestoft specialized in producing locally-commissioned pieces, with names and dates included on request. One such mug is decorated with a view of a bathing machine on the beach at Lowestoft and is inscribed, 'A Trifle from Lowestoft'. Great fun, but hardly a cheap seaside souvenir, it sold in 1983 for £5,500. Lowestoft porcelain, although crude in comparison to Worcester, commands a great following among collectors today, and unusual pieces are much sought-after. Lowestoft has a very distinctive style and this is where its charm lies.

By the late 1760s, Lowestoft drifted away from individual designs and shapes and turned increasingly to producing exact copies of Worcester. Sauceboats, oval tureens, and butter tubs are amongst some of the shapes reproduced during the 1770s. Some painted patterns were imitated, but it is mostly the transfer prints which were so faithfully copied. The Lowestoft body is much thicker and more opaque than Worcester's and the quality, particularly of the printing

ABOVE *A fine water bottle made at Philip Christian's Liverpool factory, the fancy chinoiserie design producing a splendid piece of porcelain; 28 cm (11 in), 1765-1768.*

FAR RIGHT *Lowestoft specialized in items of local interest such as this mug showing a bathing machine on the beach; 14 cm (5½ in), c.1770.*

is generally far inferior. There is great difficulty in identifying these copies today – as indeed there was in the eighteenth century – because most Lowestoft copies employed a fake crescent mark. The difference between Lowestoft copies and Worcester originals lies in the mark; whereas the legitimate Worcester crescent was a finely hatched printed mark, the Lowestoft copy was always painted open. It is surprising how often, despite the differences, Lowestoft wares are nowadays mistaken for Worcester.

There are more collectors of blue and white than of any other eighteenth-century English porcelain. A great deal of blue and white is sold at auction every year and, of course, there are the exceptional items which fetch thousands of pounds. Many pieces, however, are remarkably inexpensive. Shown here is a Christian Liverpool water bottle which had been bought as Chinese early one Friday morning at Bermondsey market. It was brought straight to Phillips, where I recognized the maker and thought the pattern looked familiar. By that same afternoon I had traced the source print to *The Ladies Amusement*, a book of engravings published by a London bookseller in the 1760s and intended to appeal particularly to ceramic decorators. The print was based on a drawing by Jean Pillemont, a French artist who, more than anyone else, influenced so much English chinoiserie. The bottle sold six weeks later, in the summer of 1988 for £1,370. The vendor was delighted, although I felt that this was ridiculously cheap for a fairly significant piece of Liverpool porcelain.

Transfer-printed Pennington or Worcester teabowls and saucers of the 1770s are often cheap; typical Christian Liverpool or Lowestoft or painted Worcester specimens are also reasonable. Early Chaffers Liverpool, Lowestoft before 1765 and Bow and Worcester before 1760 are more valuable, while rarer makers such as Vauxhall, Newcastle-under-Lyme, or Samuel Gilbody will be very expensive.

If you just wish to collect examples of the different factories, odd cups offer considerable scope and are always cheap if they are common examples or rarer damaged pieces. Gathering together examples of the various factories is really the only way to learn the difference between the pastes and glazes; fortunately this is still possible if you do not mind collecting slightly damaged pieces to begin with. Moreover, you can collect the blue and white of different factories and display pieces together without them clashing. I remember seeing the extensive collection formed by Gilbert Bradley in his London apartment. Rarely paying more than a few pounds for any piece – before blue and white was seriously collected – he gathered hundreds of pieces, including many rarities. Much of it was damaged in some way, but this did not seem to lessen the effect of the pieces displayed *en masse*. The collection added greatly to our knowledge of English blue and white, and when it was sold by Christie's in 1980, the damaged pieces were just as much in demand, in their own way, as the perfect rarities.

Chapter Six
The Golden Age

ABOVE *A Worcester plate painted in the Giles workshop. The slightly raised pattern of rose leaves is known as 'Blind Earl' after the Earl of Coventry, who lost his sight in a hunting accident and wanted a design he could feel; 19 cm (7½ in), 1765-1770.*

Such a title can be open to very many interpretations, but to me the decade from 1765 to 1775 represents the 'Golden Age' of English porcelain. It was a time during which the principal factories had overcome their initial experimentation, had created profitable markets for their wares and, with an air of confidence, could concentrate on quality unrestrained by commericial pressures. They were making their 'bread and butter' blue and white wares which paid the wages and could, therefore, afford to subsidize the manufacture of special pieces which could be kept until they found a buyer. It seems, however, that in a great many instances there was no shortage of buyers amongst the wealthy nobility. They were prepared to order the top quality pieces, whatever the cost.

Undoubtedly, the finest porcelain was expensive then, just as today the top range of Royal Worcester, Royal Crown Derby and similar contemporary wares are highly priced. Today fetching hundreds or even thousands of pounds for the best examples, eighteenth century Worcester tearwares or Derby figures may seem expensive. The chances are, though, that in real terms they cost their original owners much more in 1770. If you consider the buying power of money, and the average wages then compared with today, £134 paid in 1770 for a rich Chelsea dessert service of 41 pieces, £8.10s. for a set of large Worcester vases, or £2 for pairs of small Chelsea figures, are fairly high sums to pay. Perhaps more significant would be the cost of reproducing such workmanship today. If the present-day Worcester factory manufactured a plate like the one shown in the fine collection on page 57, the cost of the scalework ground, the bird painting, and the hand gilding would amount to at least £2,000 in order to be economical. The eighteenth-century original, today, costs less than half that amount. How ridiculous this seems! Are the modern production costs of fine hand-work vastly over-priced, or are the prices paid for the eighteenth-century pieces too cheap? This is a question worth considering.

In comparison with the blue and white wares, which were cheap to produce – yet are highly collectable and relatively expensive today – the richest coloured pieces are inexpensive considering the degree of workmanship involved. Some of these items may appear over decorated and would not appeal to everybody, but nobody can fail to marvel at the skill which went into their creation. It is difficult to conceive a factory with the technology of the 1770s actually turning out the pair of vases shown on page 55. How did Chelsea manage to fire a figure group 76 cm tall (30 inches), and very heavy, not just once, but at least five times, without it splitting or breaking apart? The factories enjoyed none of the benefits of modern electric tunnel kilns, but relied on great brick bottle kilns, the coal shovelled in by hand, the temperatures controlled only by the keen senses and experience of the kiln-man in charge of the firing for thirty hours at a time. On a simpler scale, the ability to make a cup and saucer like the ones illustrated here, perfectly potted and fired six times without a blemish, would be a remarkable feat even today. In 1765 this was miraculous, and yet Worcester and the other factories were doing this every week of the year.

BELOW *Three Worcester teabowls and saucers, and an identical teacup, all of the highest quality, 1765-1770. Relatively inexpensive and well worth collecting.*

So much was made during this period that is worthy of illustration that it has been a difficult task making a choice. The pieces that I have selected are among the highlights of the decade – although of varying quality – and it is worth explaining why each has been chosen.

A major change in styles had occurred since the 1750s when English porcelain was directly influenced by the Chinese and by Meissen. The taste for oriental wares began to mix Chinese, Japanese, and formal Meissen styles, combining them all into a style known as 'Japan'. Meanwhile, a completely different adaptation of the rococo in porcelain was introduced to England from France. This brought a new look even to simple flower painting and, above all, introduced a new world of colour to English porcelain.

Porcelain had always been favoured by the French court, but it held a particular appeal for Madame de Pompadour. She took a keen personal interest in the new factory founded at Vincennes in the late 1740s and encouraged its transfer to Sèvres in 1752. It was at Sèvres during the 1750s and 1760s that some of the most beautiful porcelain ever made was created for the King, for his own use at Court and for diplomatic gifts. Some pieces found their way to England and, suddenly, the white floral styles of Chelsea during the Red Anchor period and of Worcester seemed dreadfully dull.

The difference between Sèvres porcelain and what had preceded it lay in the new use of flowing rococo shapes and strong colours to set off the panels and produce a background for fine painting. Several ground colours were introduced from Sèvres, the most notable being a deep blue, known in France as *Bleu de Roi* and in England as 'mazarine blue'. This was painted underneath the glaze and produced a stunning rich ground which proved to be very popular. However, this blue was very hard to control and frequently

BELOW *Worcester's blue ground colour was as famous in the eighteenth century as it is today. This fine collection shows the range of decoration used to fill the panels, 1765-1775.*

ABOVE *The intense strength of Chelsea's 'mazarine blue' ground is broken up by bird panels and rococo gilding, but the effect is still rather overpowering. 37 cm (14½ in), gold anchor mark, c.1765.*

became streaky or dribbled and blurred, spoiling the reserved panels.

To overcome the problem, the English factories tried to break up the intense blue without losing its striking effect. At Bow and Worcester the cobalt oxide was applied as a fine powder, producing a mottled effect which had been popular on Chinese porcelain. This worked well as a background to blue and white panels, but lacked the dazzling effect of mazarine blue. Much more successful was a method devised at Worcester of painting small fish-scales in underglaze blue, as a background to rococo mirror-shaped panels. The curious effect this created was clearly very popular and vast quantities must have been produced – from small teawares to large sets of covered vases. The panels were usually painted with colourful flowers or a particular design of fanciful birds – known as 'fabulous' or 'dishevelled' birds – in rich vegetation. The blue ground was edged with very intricate gold rococo scrollwork and altogether the effect was splendid. Another method of breaking up the ground was to use a fine powdered cobalt which gave a soft mottled effect. The collection on page 57 is particularly clear and includes a fine example of a

Worcester teapot, a superbly balanced shape which pours beautifully and is finished off with a flower as a knob. When it was first made it was probably too costly to be used, and would have been treasured by each successive owner. Consequently, fine pieces like this are more likely to have survived in fine condition than ordinary blue and white, which would have been used more regularly.

Illustrated on page 55 are two very different styles made at Worcester at the same time as the blue ground teapot, both in the most opulent taste. The vases basically copy a Chinese *famille verte* design from the early-eighteenth century. The colours, however, have been altered with the use of an altogether brighter palette inspired by Meissen. The pattern, known at the time as 'Dragon in

LEFT *A pair of Derby figures combining a typically English shepherd and shepherdess with chinioserie arbours, the two styles mixing well; 36 cm (14¼ in), c.1770.*

Compartments' but nowadays called 'Bengal Tiger', is probably the most splendid of the Chinese-style patterns. It belongs not so much in a Chinese palace as in an English country house. The vases sold in 1985 for £12,650 – in this case considerably more than the original cost – but they are a style which very much suits the taste of modern decorators, an important factor in determining their value.

The vases are photographed alongside a dish from the most lavish of all Worcester services made in about 1770. Marked with a crescent in gold, the service was made for the Duke of Gloucester, and the novel style of fruit painting closely copies Sèvres.

However, not all of Worcester's best wares from this period need cost the buyer such sums. The three cups and saucers illustrated on page 56 were all sold in 1988 for between £250 and £330. They are examples of the different use of underglaze blue grounds and reserved panels in an oriental rococo style. Kakiemon motifs were adopted and embellished in a manner unique to Worcester. For a factory that specialized in tewares these top quality examples are not at all expensive, and combined with reasonably priced blue and white wares could form a very representative collection of cups and saucers.

Top quality Chelsea from the later 1760s is much harder to find than Worcester. The triumphs of Chelsea during the Gold Anchor period are vases inspired by the excesses of Sèvres – fanciful rococo shapes either in mazarine blue or claret grounds, reserved with panels of figure subjects inspired by Watteau and Boucher. These cost large sums when they were made, and incredible prices were paid for them early this century by wealthy collectors in England and the United States. The market for Gold Anchor Chelsea became totally unreasonable and it eventually collapsed. By the 1970s prices were less than they had been sixty years earlier. They have increased a little, and the values today probably reflect more realistically the ware's artistic merit. I have to admit that in terms of quality and taste Sèvres was far superior, although these Chelsea pieces do stand out amongst their counterparts in England.

Chelsea, Derby and Bow competed with each other to make the finest and most splendid figure groups. There is an enormous difference between English figures from the 1750s and those made in 1770. Plain mound bases which had been ornamented with lightly modelled scrollwork were replaced with heavy rococo bases, raised on scrolling legs. Sparsely modelled flowers erupted into a profusion of leaves and blossoms, known as *bocage*. Generally, the scale of these figures moved with the times, with buyers wanting value and size for their money. The customer could choose between small models of animals or large groups of, for example, eight figures dancing around a tree. While some figures are relatively simple affairs, it is worth remembering that more elaborate extremes of rococo more typically reflect the period.

There was not really a great deal of difference between the main factories at this time, except perhaps in the colouring of the figures. Bow, in particular, favoured much heavier, opaque colours, whereas Derby was still bright but tended towards the pastels. These colourings were at their best when used on figures in costumes. This gave the painter the greatest opportunity to use various colour combinations, highlighted with gold. The days of Chelsea taking pride in the whiteness of the porcelain were long gone by the 1770s, and every inch of the figure was smothered in richness. This was what the public wanted and the manufacturers were happy to oblige.

Many of the richest Bow wares and groups are marked with an anchor and dagger in red. This has been the subject of much speculation and could relate to an enamelling works in London, at Kentish Town and subsequently at Soho, under the direction of James Giles. Giles decorated Chinese porcelain and some Bow, but it was during the decade 1765-1775 that he became involved with Worcester. He worked as a china dealer in London, buying decorated Worcester at auction for resale. From the factory he was supplied directly with white glazed porcelain for his own enamelling kilns. His relationship with the Worcester factory frequently seemed strained; nevertheless, James Giles and his studio painted a great deal of Worcester porcelain, as well as some Derby, Caughley, and a large quantity of glass ware.

Based in London rather than Worcester, Giles was closer and more in tune with what the customers wanted. He painted Japanese and Chinese patterns just as the factory had done, and it is virtually impossible to tell the London and Worcester decorated wares apart. The European styles are much more distinctive, and a science has developed in recognizing the characteristics which distinguish the pieces painted in London. Certain types of birds in rich vegetation – much stonger in colour and more robust in execution – are a hallmark of Giles, together with a fairly free style of flower painting which is much livelier than the more formal style used by the factory at Worcester. One type of decoration with bird panels, deep blue grounds, and bright, flat gilding exclusive to Giles, is known as 'Lady Mary Wortley Montagu' type, after a set once owned by the Montagu family. Some of Giles's account books survive at the Victoria and Albert Museum, London, and provide some insight into the kind of work the artist was doing. It is worth studying Gerald Coke's book on Giles in order to try to recognize Giles's work, as there is little doubt that an attribution to this artist adds greatly to the price of a piece. Two words of warning, though: Giles was not the only independent decorator of porcelain in London, and it is not safe to assume that all uncharacteristic painting on Worcester must be by him. In addition, a number of pieces with Giles-type decoration appear to have been re-decorated, either at the time or at a later date, in order to make them richer and more valuable than they would otherwise have been. These pieces are discussed in Chapter 14, in the section on fakes.

ABOVE *A pair of Chelsea figures made during the Gold Anchor period, c.1765. The English rococo is seen here at its most flamboyant.*

Chapter Seven

New Developments and New Markets

During the 1760s as the quality of English porcelain generally improved, there were few significant technical changes. Methods of moulding, enamelling, and firing had been developed during the early years of the factories and most had successful recipes for their porcelain and glazes. Worcester's body had remained unchanged, and as long as the supply of soaprock lasted there was no need to improve on such a perfect formula. Bow and Lowestoft remained more or less unchanged, while Derby had improved its glazing. Chelsea, on the other hand, had let its quality slip considerably. Their best pieces showed what they were capable of, but heavy competition from Worcester and Derby forced them to economize on a certain range of items. During the Gold Anchor period of the 1760s they produced a thick glaze which was prone to 'crazing' – a network of fine cracks in the surface – and there was a greater tendency for the wares to stain. Chelsea's better pieces were marked with the anchor in gold, while the inferior wares had a brown anchor. Some of these brown anchor pieces have not stood the passage of time very well and are often heavily discoloured, with the enamel badly flaked – a sad reminder of Chelsea's decline. Sprimont had lost interest, and by 1770 ownership of the factory had transferred to William Duesbury, who ran the Derby works. He kept the Chelsea concern open and produced wares similar to those made at Derby. The term 'Chelsea-Derby' refers to the products of the two factories during this period and will be discussed further in the next chapter.

Chelsea was not the only factory to fall on hard times. Longton Hall found its unusual and exciting shapes insufficient to save the works from severe financial hardship, closing in 1760. William Littler, the proprietor, moved to West Pans near Musselburgh in Scotland, probably because coal and labour were cheaper there. The quality of the products was very poor and West Pans is not a factory of which many collectors can be proud.

England was not as advanced as Europe in producing a pure white porcelain to rival or better the Chinese. The soft paste formulae used by all of the different factories produced wares which lacked the appearance of fineness. Experiments to improve manufacturing methods revolved around attempts to imitate the hard paste formulae used by the Germans and, indeed, the Chinese, who made true porcelain using china clay or kaolin.

The principal differences between the soft or artificial pastes and true hard paste is the use of kaolin and the different firing method. The soft pastes matured in the biscuit kiln; in other words, the porcelain was fired to a high temperature first of all, causing it to vitrify and become translucent. It was only then that it could be painted in blue and glazed, and fired at a lower temperature to melt

LEFT *A water bottle made by William Littler at West Pans in Scotland; 25 cm (10 in), c.1766. This should be compared with the Liverpool bottle of similar date (page 52) to show how unsuccessful was the West Pans porcelain.*

the glaze onto the surface. Hard paste porcelain matured in the gloss kiln, with the glaze applied directly to the dry or underfired body, which was then fired at a higher temperature, to mature and vitrify the body and simultaneously seal the surface with melted glaze. Hard pastes are generally more durable and whiter, although much more difficult to control during firing.

Large deposits of china clay and china stone – the natural kaolin with feldspar needed to make porcelain – occur in Cornwall, and these were discovered by William Cookworthy, a chemist who had a keen interest in porcelain manufacture. He had tried to obtain

RIGHT A Bristol vase in hard paste porcelain, inspired by both Worcester porcelain and Sèvres, painted by 'Mons. Soqui', 1770-1772, 39.5 cm (15½ in).

suitable raw materials from Carolina and Virginia during the 1740s, but his trials using American clay were not successful. Instead, he experimented with the Cornish stone and clay and eventually discovered the secret of porcelain making. It was not, however, until 1768 that he was ready to patent his process and begin manufacture in Plymouth.

The Plymouth factory lasted only until 1770, when it was transferred to new, larger premises at Bristol. A newly formed company included Richard Champion, who took over the patent for making the hard porcelain when Cookworthy retired from the

business, now based in the Bristol premises, in 1773.

During the 1770s, some fine porcelain was made at Bristol, although Champion's lack of experience led to many problems and often incurred heavy kiln losses. His rights to the exclusive use of Cornish clay were challenged by Josiah Wedgwood in the House of Lords, and the patent became more or less worthless, although it had been financially disastrous for some time. By 1778 the business was bankrupt and the last sale of Cookworthy's true porcelain was the clearance of old stock in 1783.

The wares of Plymouth and Bristol are unmistakable with their hard, grey appearance and very tightly fitting glaze, fired at the same time as the body. The most distinctive feature is so-called 'spiral wreathing', a pattern of fine grooves which appeared on the surface of the vessels as they twisted in the intense heat of the kiln. At its best, Bristol porcelain is as white as Meissen, and indeed the crossed swords of Meissen were copied directly by Bristol. Often, though, the glaze fired a muddy grey colour and many of the earlier Plymouth wares have a very heavily speckled glaze, as if the surface were being viewed through smoke and grit.

Meissen was an important influence on Bristol, although by the

ABOVE *A collection of Bristol cups and saucers in the Meissen style, c.1775. The classical influence is also seen on the Chelsea-Derby sucrier of the same period.*

ABOVE. *The elegant simplicity of a Bristol cream jug in neo-classical style contrasted with a poor rococo shape made at Derby slightly earlier, 1770-1775.*

RIGHT *A figure group modelled by John Toulouse at Plymouth; 14.5 cm (5¾ in), c.1770. The base relates to his earlier work at Bow, although the hard paste body produces a different effect.*

1770s classical styles tended to replace the floral rococo forms. From French porcelain came inspiration for a number of pretty border patterns of flower festoons, ribbons, and emblems painted in colours or monochrome. The vase shown on the cover of this book was made at Bristol in 1770-1772 under the direction of Cookworthy and shows the Sèvres influence in the painting, on what is basically a Worcester shape. It is believed to be by a former Worcester painter, 'Mons. Soqui', although little is known about this artist's life. The Bristol factory had placed advertisements in the Worcester newspapers in 1770 asking for painters, and a number of hands seen on Bristol wares were undoubtedly also at Worcester. The known examples of Plymouth blue and white are unquestionably by former Worcester painters who responded to the advertisement. These blue and white wares were largely discontinued after the move to Bristol, as the cobalt used at Plymouth fired to such an unnatural grey-black colour.

Modest figure subjects were modelled by John Toulouse, who began his career as a modeller at Bow and then went to Worcester. He produced a very similar style of figure at Bristol, but his skills were far inferior to the Derby modellers during the 1770s and his pieces were not terribly successful. Much more successful were certain unglazed white biscuit porcelain plaques of finely modelled flowers which were unique to the factory.

The hard paste formula at Plymouth and Bristol, then, cannot really be classed as a success. Certain fine pieces did emerge, but, generally, the wares were mediocre and disappointing, and it is not surprising that Champion finally went into bankruptcy.

The market for English porcelain changed significantly in the 1770s. In addition to cheaper oriental wares, the porcelain makers were faced with new competiton from the potters of Staffordshire and northern England. Earthenware potters had developed a material called creamware which, although not translucent like porcelain, could be thinly moulded and was well suited to making teapots and dinnerwares. Josiah Wedgwood was able to market his creamware very successfully in London, where he called it 'Queensware', and he made his services more fashionable than porcelain. Another threat to porcelain was pearlware, which the potters achieved by adding a touch of blue colouring to the body. Pearlware could be just as thin as porcelain and could be decorated with underglaze blue painting and printing, which enabled it to compete favourably with the Chinese wares. The blue and white porcelains made at Worcester, Bow, and Lowestoft were seriously affected by these new wares and all of the factories faced periods of falling sales and hardship.

Bow was ultimately forced to close and production stopped in about 1770. Lowestoft survived, but relied on local trade for special orders, with production very much reduced. Liverpool, too, saw factories closing. The quality of the porcelain made there deteriorated just as the standard of creamware decorated in Liverpool greatly improved. The porcelain manufacturers had to find a way of competing with the cheaper wares, to avoid being driven out of business.

Probably the most successful factory was established in around

1772 by Thomas Turner, who had been an important manager at Worcester. He had trained under Robert Hancock as a master engraver, and he seems to have been able to persuade Hancock to join him in a new venture in the village of Caughley, in Shropshire. New kilns were built in the middle of the countryside, far inland from the waterways on which other makers depended. Local coal and labour were cheap and plentiful, and usable clay was also abundant. Turner was a shrewd businessman and he looked for a gap in the market which he could fill. He knew from his position at Worcester the secrets of the soaprock body, and at the same time he knew where to obtain the necessary raw materials. His experience at Worcester was

RIGHT *A Liverpool coffee pot from Pennington's factory, 32 cm (12½ in), c.1780. The decoration copies cheap exported Chinese porcelains of the same period.*

in the blue and white department; it was in this area that he targeted his new venture.

Production of expensive coloured wares and figures had eventually brought ruin to Chelsea and to Bow. At Worcester profit was made not from the fine enamelled wares but from the common blue and white. Turner's departure must have been a severe blow to Worcester as he undoubtedly took other workmen with him, as well as a knowledge of the tastes of the factory's customers. Turner had no desire to make coloured wares and, instead, had by 1775 established the most efficient factory in the country for making blue-printed porcelain.

I do not believe Thomas Turner brought any actual engraved copper printing plates with him to Caughley, but he soon set about creating new ones, exactly copying all the best selling designs used at Worcester. The Worcester works had already lost many of their best blue and white painters to Plymouth and Derby in 1770. This had come about as a result of Worcester developing printing techniques, but the concentration on printing backfired when Turner began imitating them. They now had to struggle to compete and by the 1780s there is no doubt that Caughley were completely dominating the market for blue and white and Worcester were in trouble.

Caughley (pronounced car-flee) achieved dominance in two ways. First, they concentrated on the saleable product and did not attempt any coloured or gilded wares. Second, they mass-produced

ABOVE *A collection of Caughley blue and white porcelain, 1775-1790. The popular 'Fisherman' pattern is seen in a particularly fine mask-spouted jug; 22 cm (8½ in).*

simple shapes and very elaborate blue and white printed patterns, which the public wanted to buy, at competitive prices. Salopian china, named after the Latin for Shropshire, soon gained a reputation as the best ordinary porcelain available, competing favourably with Staffordshire and Leeds pearlware. Having virtually destroyed his main rival's trade in blue and white, Turner did not rest. Instead he persuaded the Worcester factory's chief decorators, Robert and Humphrey Chàmberlain, to leave their employers and start up on their own as painters and gilders, decorating blank porcelain sent to Worcester from Caughley. From about 1786 until 1793 the Chamberlains added gilding to blue and white Caughley and enamelled special pieces to order. The dessert set made for the Marquis of Donegal, and shown here, is a superb example of one of these special commissions.

Dr Wall had retired from the Worcester factory in 1775 and died in Bath in the following year. William Davis struggled to keep the factory afloat against all odds, and was joined in 1783 by the business acumen of John Flight. During the Davis-Flight period some blue and white which could compete with Caughley was produced. However, mostly as a result of poor control of printing and firing, the Worcester pieces tended to be of an inferior quality. To avoid these problems, they copied some Caughley patterns by hand; but the time involved must have made this quite uneconomical. By

BELOW *A Caughley dessert service decorated by Chamberlain in Worcester for the Marquis of Donegal in 1793. The service is 'harlequin', each piece decorated with a different border.*

the time of the arrival at Worcester of a new partner, Martin Barr, in 1793, all blue and white production at the factory had ceased.

It has been estimated that there are more collectors of Caughley than any other single eighteenth-century factory. The reason for this is the relative cheapness and the fact that the wares are easily recognized and frequently in good condition. The factory's specialities are not the most expensive. Taste had changed by the 1780s and the public preferred all-over decoration. The Chinese painted incredibly complicated landscape scenes and Caughley fought back with cheaper transfer prints. It has often been argued that Thomas Turner introduced at Caughley the first use of the 'Willow' pattern – a very well-known design, inspired by the Chinese, and yet quintessentially English. Although probably in use on Staffordshire pearlware by 1790, the 'Willow' pattern as such was never used on porcelain. Instead, Caughley used related, complex chinoiserie landscapes, with figures on bridges, fancy temples, and willow trees within particularly ornate borders. These wares are not so fashionable nowadays and are probably undervalued. Other Caughley wares, decorated in distinctive deep blue and gold patterns or just bright gilding are certainly worth watching out for.

In far greater demand from Caughley are pretty shapes, of which the factory made a great number. These include all manner of tablewares, such as creamboats, mustard pots and small wine tasters.

BELOW *A Caughley miniature teaset made as a child's plaything, c.1785. The milk jug is only 5 cm (2 in) high.*

Asparagus servers were wedge-shaped holders for serving fresh asparagus, and egg drainers were small saucer-shaped trays pierced with holes and fitted with a small handle. Examples of these, and a variety of leaf or shell-shaped pickle dishes can make a fascinating collection.

Caughley made a large number of miniature items, teawares, and dinnerwares, perfectly scaled down and sold in the eighteenth century as 'toys'. They were just that: expensive playthings for fortunate children, or novelties for adults to collect. Their rarity and appealing charm make these 'toys' much more valuable than the actual full-sized wares. A miniature Caughley chamberpot that had been bought in a car boot sale for 25 pence was sold in 1986 for £1,370 and, while this was a particularly rare shape, it does illustrate that collecting miniatures is certainly not child's play nowadays. A point worth mentioning is that miniature porcelain pieces were never intended to be 'traveller's samples' as is commonly believed.

While Caughley acquired a virtual monopoly over the production of blue and white English porcelain, they made very few coloured wares. Instead, serious competition for the *famille rose* patterns from China came not from Worcester and Bristol, but from Staffordshire. William Littler, who had failed at Longton Hall and West Pans, returned to Staffordshire in the 1770s and formed a partnership with John Baddeley to produce a very different sort of ware – much more delicate and prettier than anything previously made in Staffordshire. Their successors, Baddeley, Booth & Co., probably produced great quantities of teawares, although these wares are frequently confused with the most important of the Staffordshire porcelain makers, the New Hall factory in Shelton, Stoke-on-Trent.

RIGHT *An early New Hall creamboat identified by its characteristic 'clip' handle; 11 cm (4¹/₄ in) long, c.1782. In spite of a chip it sold in 1988 for £600, evidence of its rarity.*

There is much confusion about the early years of New Hall and any connection with Richard Champion at Bristol. Champion was hopeful of finding a buyer for his patent to manufacture true porcelain, following the bankruptcy of the Bristol works. He visited Staffordshire in 1781 and spent five months at the New Hall factory trying to make a successful hard paste body. It is likely that nothing came of this, as Champion left at about the same time as production began of an entirely new porcelain body by the business partnership at New Hall. Although often called hard paste, New Hall porcelain is quite different from the true porcelain of Germany or China. Nowadays, a term used in connection with New Hall is 'hybrid paste', a complicated name for a body that is really neither hard nor soft paste. The New Hall body can exhibit signs of spiral wreathing, but is of a grey-green tint rather than pure white. Like Bristol, New Hall's glaze can sometimes appear very smoky, but its body is very strong and durable, very well-suited to the manufacture of tewares.

From the outset, New Hall specialized in tea services, to the exclusion of virtually everything else. It aimed its products not at the wealthy gentry, but more at the middle classes. The factory used new production methods applied to an extensive range of patterns, mostly inspired by Chinese export porcelain. They copied many of the simple patterns which were imported in bulk from China, in particular the formal border designs in *famille rose*, a range of enamel colours including pink and puce.

An innovation at New Hall was the use of pattern numbers painted onto the porcelain. Each design was given a number rather than a name, and a simple progressive system was used, beginning with 1 and eventually exceeding 3,000 by the 1820s.

Certain patterns were more successful than others and the numbering system is extremely beneficial to collectors today.

LEFT *A Staffordshire teapot of the 1790s from a class of wares attributed to 'Factory Z'. An elegant pattern well suited to the classical shape, pattern no. 91.*

Amongst the most sought-after of the early patterns are no. 3, an early floral pattern with formal border; no. 83, with roses in gilded panels; and no. 20, a charming chinoiserie design of bubble-headed figures standing by a fence. Acquisition by pattern numbers is a very different way of forming a collection. The numbers were not, of course, developed purely for the benefit of future collectors. They enabled china dealers to re-order popular patterns and helped them to keep track of their stock. The success of this system meant that dealers encouraged other makers to adopt similar methods, especially since virtually identical shapes and patterns were made by a number of different factories.

Early collectors often confused these similar wares and any late-eighteenth century teawares in simple Chinese style were incorrectly termed New Hall. It soon became clear that some pattern numbers did not agree, and it was possible to separate other groups of wares which must have originated from other factories. Some could be identified as Coalport or Worcester, but most could not be attributed. David Holgate, who did much of the pioneering work on New Hall and its contemporaries, adopted the names 'Factory X', 'Factory Y' and 'Factory Z' for the three largest groups, and these names have been commonly adopted by collectors. Various attributions have been suggested for the 'X', 'Y' and 'Z' classes, but so far no positive identification is possible. There were a large number of other small factories making these simple teawares at the turn of the eighteenth century; a great deal of research remains to be done if some of these are to be given definite names.

It is easy to understand why the collecting of New Hall and its contemporaries is now so popular. Cups and saucers are plentiful and need not be expensive. Those identifiable as New Hall fetch anything up to twice the price of a piece bearing the same pattern, but produced by an unknown factory, although the New Hall example may not necessarily be of better quality. There can be more variety than many people think, especially if particular shapes, such as milk jugs or teapots, are sought. It is also possible to find examples of the

RIGHT *A New Hall* sucrier *painted by Fidelle Duvivier, with his distinctive curly-haired* putti; *10.5 cm, (4 in), c.1785.*

Chinese prototypes for many of the patterns. However, with so many New Hall collectors, the appearance of a particularly rare piece at auction creates considerable competition and prices are high. The most sought-after are pieces painted by Fidelle Duvivier, whose work for New Hall was in total contrast to the rest of their production. He painted individual scenes in colours and monochrome, in a continental style reminiscent of early Chelsea. Duvivier's landscapes frequently featured scenes of the potteries, with smoking bottle kilns very much in evidence. The sucrier illustrated opposite shows his typical curly-haired children. This sold in 1981 for £2,100 and will be worth considerably more today. It represents, however, the exception rather than the rule for New Hall, as the factory did not generally produce individually designed pieces, leaving this area to other manufacturers.

Competition from factories geared to mass-production seriously affected the large established firms. There is no doubt that Caughley and New Hall, combined with Chinese imports and Staffordshire creamware, dealt a severe blow to Worcester and Derby in the 1780s. Worcester had always aimed its products at the top end of the market, subsidized by more ordinary wares and its blue and white. They found, however, that they could no longer manufacture for both markets, as Caughley and New Hall, without the overheads of the glamorous wares, easily undercut them on the cheaper wares. A choice had to be made between switching to mass-production or relying solely on the finer wares to support the business.

relying solely on the finer wares to support the business.

Thankfully, both Worcester and Derby realized that there would always be a market for the best that money could buy, and so they concentrated on high quality wares rather than give in to commercial pressures calling for cheaper and cheaper products. They were happy to let the Staffordshire potters take over the market for simple wares and, instead, concentrated on quality.

ABOVE *Two New Hall teapots in the style of Chinese Export wares, 1785-1790. Produced inexpensively in complete contrast to the grander wares of Worcester and Derby.*

Chapter Eight
The Classical Revival and Regency Styles

By the late 1770s, largely due to the marketing skills of Josiah Wedgwood, London customers no longer wanted fancy rococo designs. Classical styles came back into fashion, and followers of the neo-classical taste, with its Adams-style decoration and furniture, wanted a new kind of elegance in their porcelain. Wedgwood had styled his 'Queensware' with dramatic, formal borders; this reserved elegance, as opposed to all-over richness, gradually spread to porcelain design.

Derby had maintained a presence in London following the collapse of Chelsea, and the period known as Chelsea-Derby during the 1770s was increasingly reliant on classical designs. Plates and dishes were painted with urns hung with swags of flowers, and

BELOW *A Worcester dessert dish painted in London in the new classical style of the 1770s, a very different effect to the other more lavish porcelain decorated in the Giles workshop; 26 cm (10¼ in)*, Dyson Perrins Museum.

Grecian-style borders, festoons of husks linking rams' heads and wheel medallions, known as patterae, completed a new symmetrical elegance more suited to porcelain than the hardness of creamware. Vase shapes copied Roman originals instead of Chinese or French, and figure groups were based on the work of such artists as Angelica Kaufmann. Gods and mortals in an appealing range of soft pastel colours were contrasted with white porcelain and a brilliant turquoise blue enamel.

Good neo-classical English porcelain is surprisingly hard to find, and certainly Derby led the field. James Giles's workshop in London in the 1770s adopted the new style and he painted on Worcester blanks, dessert services with borders of vines and flowers and central marble vases. The Worcester factory itself was slow to catch on to the new style, although a few classical designs were made in the later 1770s, particularly in black enamel or in gold on elegant tea services. Aimed at the London market, it is difficult to tell if these were actually painted at the factory or decorated in London.

The classical taste remained most suited to pottery, however, and Wedgwood, with his 'Jasperware' and imitation stone effects, continued to dominate. The porcelain makers looked to France once again for inspiration; the simple patterns with rich formal gilding, which were Paris's answer to the neo-classical movement, had more

BELOW *Two Worcester tea canisters of 1775-1780 with fine enamelled and gilded husks and patterae. Neo-classical porcelain at its most successful.* Dyson Perrins Museum.

direct influence on English porcelain than the true classical antiquities reproduced by Wedgwood for the Adamesque interiors of country houses. Joseph Flight travelled to France in the 1780s and was clearly very much taken with the latest French styles, which he felt must be the only way ahead for his own struggling Worcester porcelain factory.

By the time Martin Barr joined Flight as co-director of the Worcester factory in 1793, the production of ordinary blue and white wares had stopped. Instead the decision was made to concentrate on high quality pieces. This did not necessarily mean that production would be limited only to very expensive items. Flight and Barr wanted to regain the factory's former position as a leading force in the London market, and this meant keeping up with the current tastes. Under Flight's direction the original soaprock recipe had been improved and the quality of the factory's tea services had never been higher in terms of eggshell thinness and translucence, as well as control in the kilns. Spiral fluted shapes were all the rage in the late 1780s, and the Flight factory's quality of potting was superior to that of its rivals.

BELOW *A Worcester plate from the Duke of Clarence service ordered in 1789, 24.3 cm (9½ in), the quality deserving of a royal service.*

The factory had also re-discovered the art of fine gilding. They had suffered a setback in 1787 when the Chamberlains, who had been in charge of most of the factory's decorating, suddenly left to form their own workshop for the Caughley factory. Flight had to employ new artists and learn the secrets of gilding almost from scratch, but, by 1790, had succeeded. By this time the Chamberlains had begun to manufacture their own porcelain and severed their links with Caughley. Because of their background, the products of the Flight and Barr and the Chamberlain factories, on opposite sides of the cathedral in Worcester, were remarkably similar during the 1790s. Flight's were well ahead in quality at the upper end of the market, but very similar teawares were made by the two firms, in spiral fluted shapes decorated in underglaze blue with gold, or just with simple gold sprigs. At the lower end of the scale, Chamberlain's made wares similar in quality to those of New Hall and other Staffordshire factories, in total contrast to Flight and Barr.

Towards the end of the eighteenth century there were really only two factories competing for the top end of the market. The wealthy gentry wanting a new service to impress their friends would

BELOW *A Chamberlain tea service of spiral-fluted shape from the 1790s. The gilded decoration is elegant and was very popular at the time, although it is inexpensive today.*

choose between Derby and Flight and Barr. Royal patronage was very important and both factories competed for special royal orders. In 1789 the Duke of Clarence chose Worcester to produce the magnificent service that celebrated his new title of Duke of St

Andrew. Critics complained about the strong and exaggerated colouring and felt that the blue and green did not work well together, but the effect is certainly stunning. Still in use at Windsor, the service was an important milestone in the factory's history. A single plate, shown on page 78, sold at Phillips in 1988 for £5,500, and it is easy to understand why. In 1789 the Duke wanted a new dinner and dessert service; in complete contrast to the armorial set, he commissioned a set decorated with painted scenes, allegories of Hope. Derby and Worcester each prepared specimens designed by their top artists and the Duke chose which he liked best. Once again, Flight's won the order for their design of a rich underglaze blue and gold border and paintings in sepia monochrome by their top figure painter, John Pennington. When finally completed, the service was put on exhibition in London and won considerable acclaim for the factory, as well as many new orders.

Flight and Barr had found their market and now knew how to be successful. Their more ordinary tea services were all finished off with gold: quality was now the prime consideration. They saw no need to compete with New Hall and others in Staffordshire and instead kept the nobility and gentry supplied with simple patterns or more elaborate designs, depending on their taste.

Derby had a softer, creamy glaze which made the contrasted monochrome and gold patterns used by Flight's less appropriate. Instead, they used coloured enamels to great effect and, like their rival, Derby concentrated above all on the quality of their products. They specialized in using borders of plain colours or coloured scrollwork with central paintings by a most impressive team of artists who were capable of almost any subject. To the Derby artists the piece of porcelain became a canvas on which a miniature painting would hang, framed against a formal patterned or coloured backcloth. The painters set out to rival the European factories of Vienna, Berlin, and Sèvres, creating 'cabinet pieces' – cups and saucers so expensive they could never be used but, instead, were collected as works of art and proudly displayed in the most elegant drawing rooms.

In the 1790s Flight and Barr had only one artist capable of such work – namely John Pennington. Derby, on the other hand, could present their patrons with a choice. Landscapes were the speciality of Zachariah Boreman and Joseph Hill, equally fine painters distinguished by their different use of colours. Boreman favoured heavy blue-grey tints to his trees and fields, while Hill preferred autumn tints and washes of yellow. Two brothers, Robert and John Brewer, were versatile artists whose work ranged from landscapes and seascapes to flowers and birds. George Robertson painted fine landscapes and particularly excelled at shipping subjects on choppy seas. George Complin, a superb miniaturist, painted fruit in luscious still lifes. All the painters helped create a thriving studio at Derby and there was no shortage of customers willing to pay for their work.

One artist, however, stands out above all the others for the quality of his work and for the influence he was to have on china painting. The name of William Billingsley is synonymous with flower

LEFT *Three Derby 'Keddleston' vases in the
most elaborate neo-classical taste, the
painted landscapes by Zachariah Boreman;
23.5 cm, (9¼ in), blue painted marks.*

BELOW *A Derby 'Trio' (coffee can, teacup
and saucer) painted with shipping scenes by
George Robertson, c.1795. Traditionally
made for a Quaker family who asked for a
brown rim instead of gold.*

ABOVE *A Barr, Flight, and Barr Worcester dessert service painted by William Billingsley, c.1814. This painting is exceptional and influenced a great many china painters.*

painting. His career spanning half a century encompasses the whole field of English porcelain. It is worth recounting at some length as it sums up the period and represents the struggles which affected every manufacturer during this time.

The son of an independent china painter who had worked at Chelsea, young William Billingsley was apprenticed to William Duesbury at Derby in 1774, when he was sixteen. He spent five years learning the trade and his talents soon made him the factory's senior flower painter. His work was totally different from anything seen in England before. The formal flower painting on Chelsea and Worcester was pretty and effective, but lacked life. Billingsley developed a method of painting using thick enamels which could be textured and arranged like oil painting on canvas, the whiteness of the porcelain showing through to represent the highlights. Close up, the painting seems to lack detail, but when viewed on a table during a meal the flowers seem so real that they jump from the dishes and you can almost smell their sweet scent. Illustrated here is an example of Billingsley's work at its best, but it has to be compared with other English flower painting of the period to appreciate just how advanced and forward-thinking it really is, in comparison.

While at Derby, Billingsley learnt the entire porcelain trade. He was capable of fine gilding and ground-lay and together with his friend, the landscape painter Zachariah Boreman, he experimented at home to learn the secrets of making porcelain. During 1795 and 1796, Billingsley painted at Derby for a full sixty hours a week and then each weekend travelled the fifteen miles to Pinxton, where he

supervised the building of kilns on the estate of John Coke, the son of a wealthy landowner. By October 1796 the new factory was ready and Billingsley left Derby to take over the running of the Pinxton china works.

Some beautiful porcelain was made at Pinxton, and pieces painted by Billingsley himself are very keenly sought by collectors. Kiln losses, however, were enormous and the venture cost a great deal of money. The last firings were in 1799 and, just three years after his arrival, Billingsley moved on to a small terraced house in Mansfield. Here he set up an enamelling kiln where he decorated white porcelain remaining from the Pinxton factory, as well as other white wares bought from Coalport, Derby, Staffordshire and even France. Producing excellent work at Mansfield, especially fine rich gilding, Billingsley still longed to make his own successful porcelain to rival the soft creamy paste of Sèvres. From 1802 Billingsley spent six years at Brampton, near Torksey in Derbyshire, where he found local finance for a further attempt at fine porcelain. It was not a success and he set out by boat for Swansea, taking his two daughters with him. His wife, Sarah, had remained in Derby since 1802 and his

ABOVE *A collection of Pinxton wares, the simple decoration mostly painted after Billingsley had left the factory, although his influence is seen in the landscape paintings.*

daughters were his only comfort as he dodged creditors under the alias William Beeley. Billingsley failed to find work in Wales and travelled instead to Worcester, finding employment at the Flight factory. He worked for Flight's for five years, initially as a painter, but subsequently he put his technical knowledge to good use and worked to perfect a new porcelain formula. In spite of large payments to protect their investment, Billingsley left the Worcester factory in 1813, returning to Wales to establish the porcelain factory based in premises in Swansea.

ABOVE *A pair of Staffordshire 'bough pots' probably painted in the Mansfield workshop of William Billingsley, 19 cm (7½ in) high, c.1800, the elaborate gilding producing a very rich effect.*

The successful products of this venture are discussed in Chapter 9. Billingsley's life, however, remained as troubled as ever. Unable to find backers, and heavily in debt, he was destitute when both of his daughters died within nine months of each other in 1817. Swansea was a financial disaster. New backers put up over £2,000 and a new factory was built at Nantgarw, again making beautiful porcelain, but also with heavy kiln losses. In 1820, for the fifth time, Billingsley deserted a bankrupt factory and set out on foot to walk the 100 miles to Coalport. He helped to improve the Coalport porcelain body, but did no further painting and died in 1828, aged 70. He was buried under the alias William Beeley, in a church near Coalport.

When you see a Derby plate with a bold flower bouquet, or a Pinxton cup and saucer with a sensitive landscape by William Billingsley, do not merely look upon them as beautiful pieces of porcelain. They represent part of the struggle to fulfil his dream, and deserve to be held in the highest esteem.

Billingsley was not the only genius who was unable to find

fulfilment in Regency England. Thomas Baxter's influence on figure and landscape painting was almost as great as Billingsley's on flower decoration, and this artist also led a troubled and unsettled life. Between 1800 and 1810 Thomas Baxter worked in his own studio in London, painting white porcelain mostly provided by Coalport. From 1811 he was in Worcester, painting and modelling for Flight's factory while running his own china painting school. He joined Billingsley at Swansea in 1816, and painted some of the finest of all the Welsh porcelain, but the factory failed and Baxter returned to

Worcester, this time to the Chamberlain factory. Here, he painted little baskets, ink-pots, and small fancy pieces until his death in 1819, at the young age of 39.

Like Billingsley before him, Thomas Baxter's method of fine stippled painting and delicate colouring influenced a great many other china painters. It can, therefore, often be very difficult to distinguish Billingsley's and Baxter's work from that of their followers. Correct attribution is very important. The pair of jardinières shown here were brought into Phillips in 1984, considered by their owner as French. I recognized the porcelain body as the granular grey of Coalport, rather than the hard whiteness of Paris, and searching closely among the rocks and drapery of the painting, I found the tiny hidden signature 'T. Baxter, 1800'. As a result, and in spite of heavy damage, the jardinières sold for £2,750. This was considerably more than they would have made had they been French.

An even more extreme example of the importance of research is the commemorative plate delivered to Phillips amongst a collection

ABOVE *Brought into Phillips as French, the hidden signature of Thomas Baxter correctly identified these* jardinières *as Coalport; 14.5 cm (5¾ in), dated 1800.*

of Nelson souvenirs. It was clearly signed 'T. Baxter, 1806', and commemorates the life and death of the great admiral. I was able to discover, however, that not only was it based on the artist's own sketches of Emma Hamilton, who appears dressed as Britannia, but that it features in a painting of Thomas Baxter's studio exhibited by the artist at the Royal Academy in 1809. The importance of the plate correctly recognized, it sold in 1983 for £11,000, an incredible price for a single plate.

Lord Nelson, himself, was a great lover of porcelain. He owned cabinet pieces by Thomas Baxter and wares from the great factories of Europe. His own taste, however, was as flamboyant as the times in which he lived. When Nelson visited Chamberlain's in Worcester in 1802, he ordered a full service of one of the factory's richest patterns, called 'Fine Old Japan'. It is a pattern which was derived from an early Japanese original, but it was enriched with stronger colours and more gold for the English taste during the Regency period. In Nelson's case he had his own coat of arms and crest added to the pattern, and the final effect, while certainly very over-the-top, must have been quite stunning when used for the very first time at his house in Merton.

BELOW *Two superb English porcelain plates*. Right: *Flight Worcester, painted by John Pennington for the Duke of Clarence, 1789;* left: *Coalport, painted by Thomas Baxter to celebrate the life of Lord Nelson, signed and dated 1806; 24 cm (9½ in)*.

The great factories of Derby, Flight, and Chamberlain led the way in the production of these rich, updated oriental styles. Known variously as 'Japan', 'Indian' or 'Imari', the patterns feature a rich, deep underglaze blue, flame orange, red and gold, with other colours added as required. Competition for this market went beyond Worcester and Derby, however, as the formal 'Japan' patterns did not require the same skills as free-hand painting. New Hall made many such patterns, including very striking designs with elephants or tigers; but by far the biggest producer was the Coalport factory.

John Rose set up his factory at Coalport on the banks of the River Severn, near Ironbridge in Shropshire, during the 1790s, and in 1799 he took over the ailing Caughley works from Thomas Turner. Both factories ran together until 1813, when the Caughley site was closed, and during this period John Rose was mass-producing tea, dessert, and dinner services, with an output much larger than any of his rivals. Wares ranged from simple coloured Chinese designs to compete with New Hall, blue and gold patterns on fluted shapes to rival both Worcester factories, sets painted with flowers after French or Dresden originals, underglaze blue prints to rival the Chinese, and very extensive services in the 'Japan' styles. Coalport's successful

BELOW *Derby is probably best known for its Imari patterns, widely used on teasets and on vases such as these, made in 1815; 22.5 cm (9 in), red painted marks.*

formula of using a limited number of plain shapes, but a very large number of different patterns, was soon to be taken up by a great many other factories.

The market for English porcelain was opening up and there was room for many more manufacturers. Chinese porcelain was considered old fashioned and its importation gradually stopped. English copies had become cheaper anyway, and French and German imports were still very restricted. Consequently, the English middle classes all wanted to buy English porcelain. In addition, the working classes found that the simpler, cottage-style wares were no longer beyond their means. The secrets of manufacture were more widely known and a great centre built up in the five pottery towns of Stoke-on-Trent, where new porcelain makers were starting businesses every month to join the even larger numbers of earthenware manufacturers.

Most of these porcelain makers developed versions of the

BELOW *A Coalport dessert service of c.1805, in rich Japan style, the most flamboyant form of decoration available at the time. The pattern was made by many English factories during the Regency period.*

hybrid paste used at New Hall and Coalport. Early in the nineteenth century factories such as Spode and Minton experimented, using very high percentages of calcined animal bones mixed with china clay and stone. By 1815, many factories were making 'bone china' which, although not as durable as the hybrid true porcelains, could be made cheaply with relatively small losses during the firings.

Directories of manufacturers in Staffordshire give a good insight into the growing number of porcelain makers, rising steadily until 1828 when Piggott & Co.'s directory lists 138 factories of which 47 were claiming to make porcelain. Of the porcelain makers, only eight regularly used any sort of factory mark on their wares, and the vast majority of English porcelain made during the first half of the nineteenth century is unmarked. Identification of pieces is made difficult because clear maker's marks do not appear on the bottom of every example. Instead, a considerable amount of detective work is necessary to tell any of the makers apart.

BELOW *A Chamberlain Worcester tureen, 39 cm (15½ in) wide, of the same Japan pattern seen on the Coalport service (opposite). When Lord Nelson visited the factory in 1803 he ordered a set of this pattern with armorial bearings.*

Chapter Nine
New French Influences

The first twenty years of the nineteenth century can be termed the era of the tea service in English porcelain. Tea had become much less expensive and was widely drunk at all levels of society. Every house needed a tea service and plenty of factories were willing to provide for this vast market. The china dealers who supplied most of these services were very skilful at promoting rapid changes of taste. If a style remained popular for along time, people would continue to use the same tea service, but if they could be persuaded that last year's set was old-fashioned and nobody was using it in the current year, they would certainly rush out to buy a new set. By repeating this ploy every few years, the china dealers maintained a steady market.

Retailers were particularly interested in keeping their customers, encouraging them to come back for additions or replacements for their services. Dealers were willing to sell the wares of any factory which would give them a reasonable discount, but they were keen to discourage customers from going direct to the makers for their china. Therefore, most shops would only carry wares which were totally unmarked. However, the important factories of Flight and Chamberlain in Worcester, Derby and Wedgwood, had their own retail outlets. They also had established reputations, so dealers would sell the wares of these factories as 'Worcester porcelain' or 'Real Derby', using the marks as proof of authenticity. Gradually, other makers built up reputations and took to marking some wares; Spode and Davenport are typical examples.

The modern collector is, therefore, faced with a terribly difficult situation. There were dozens of factories, all making the same basic shapes, changing them as frequently as the market dictated, and often using identical patterns. Only a few factories used marks at all, and, even then, only on certain wares. It is enough to make a new collector give up before he begins, but it is worth persevering, as this is where the detective work comes in. All factories made their own moulds from their own modelled prototype shapes, and there are always some differences in the angles of the handles or spouts. All the teapots of one shape from one factory will be virtually identical in form, regardless of decoration. So, a Chamberlain teapot made for Lord Nelson with full armorial bearings will be exactly the same shape as the one made at the same time for a less extravagant customer, and gilded with a simple sprig pattern. Thus, once you have identified one teapot as being by a particular factory, through a mark, handle or spout shape or through documentary evidence, then any other teapots matching it exactly must originate from the same factory.

Pattern numbers are vitally important at this stage. Most factories used them by the 1810s, and many before this time. When the same pattern is used by more than one maker, the numbers given to that pattern by each factory will be different. New Hall's pattern no. 186 is the same as pattern no. 126 in 'Factory X'. So a piece with this design, which is attributed to New Hall, must have pattern no. 186 on it or be ruled out and deemed to originate from another factory. Similarly, once you have identified a teapot as Ridgway, for example, and it bears the pattern no. 418, any other shape of teaware with the same decoration and pattern number must also be Ridgway. By this method it has been possible to identify the pattern number sequences used by many of the factories, and with these, the natural progression of shapes.

Pattern numbers were recorded in pattern books kept at the factories. Complete series of these books survive at several factories, mostly in the archives of those continuing the same tradition today. Pattern books for the Chamberlain and Grainger works survive at Worcester, but the records of Flight's factory, which did not use pattern numbers, were probably destroyed in the middle of the nineteenth century. Other books remain at Coalport, Spode, and Minton, while fragments of pattern books also survive in museums or are in private hands. These records have proved invaluable towards identifying unmarked but numbered pieces.

Most of the original research into teaware shapes was done by Geoffrey Godden and has been extended by the contributions of Philip Miller and Michael Berthoud. Their respective publications – *Staffordshire Porcelain*, *British Teapots*, and *British Cups* – are essential

BELOW *The so-called 'London' shape was made by every factory. This service is a good example of Swansea's version, combining an Imari pattern with painted flowers,* c.1816.

ABOVE *A high quality Davenport bough or bulb pot from the early days of the factory; 18.5 cm (7¼ in), c.1810. The painted panel is particularly fine.*

literature for anyone wishing to collect and identify teawares of this period, and are used continually in Phillips' porcelain department. A list of specialist books which record the shapes and pattern numbers used at individual factories is given on pages 147-151.

Collectors naturally like to identify the makers of every piece, and it is frustrating when an item is clearly of fine quality, but cannot be given an attribution other than 'Staffordshire' or 'interesting, perhaps Coalport'. Research is continuing, and a great many shapes which could not be identified when sold ten years ago are now recognized as standard. The size of the problem remaining is illustrated by the 'London' shape, which had a distinctive rounded rectangular teapot, conical cups, and hook handles. Every factory, it seems, made its own version of this shape, including Worcester and Swansea. In *British Teapots*, Miller and Berthoud illustrate more than 180 examples, and while many are attributed to one of 22 different factories, a very large number are unidentified. It will never be possible to identify them all, but there is certainly plenty of interesting work to be done and it is possible for anyone to come across a 'missing link', a marked example which puts a name to a whole unattributed group. Philip Miller himself started collecting teapots only ten years

ago and his collection numbered nearly two thousand when it was sold in 1988 to the Castle Museum in Norwich as a reference collection to help further research. Old theories, some well established, are frequently being replaced by new, more plausible explanations, and I have learnt to keep an open mind about attribution unless the evidence is conclusive.

By 1815-1820 the monopoly which Derby and Worcester had over the manufacture of rich and expensive ornamental wares had vanished. Many other makers had shown that if the customer could afford it, they had the skills to produce equally fine workmanship. The Flight factory in Worcester probably remained the most consistent leader, only producing pieces of quality through its entire history up to the 1830s. Spode, Ridgway, and Davenport all manufactured special royal commissions and rich cabinet wares, but these were made alongside cheaper earthenwares, blue printed wares and 'cottage' porcelains.

ABOVE *The quality of Derby gilding is often ignored, yet while the paintings on these pieces of c.1815-1820 are pleasant, it is the gilding which sets them above the level of other late-Regency Staffordshire porcelain.*

Derby had replaced its fine creamy porcelain with an inferior bone china and, by the 1820s, was showing signs that it could no longer match its former glory. Painting by William 'Quaker' Pegg of botanical specimens, Richard Dodson's birds and many other named artists kept the factory at the top of the decorative porcelain market, but its run-of-the-mill teawares in poor bone china were not of a similar class. Likewise, Chamberlain made some wonderfully rich painted wares – especially those outstanding examples of craftsmanship by Humphrey Chamberlain himself – but they, too, tried to compete by producing cheaper services which should really have remained the preserve of the Staffordshire factories. Chamberlain also faced home-grown competition in this area from a third Worcester factory, Grainger & Co., established across the city by Thomas Grainger who had previously worked for Chamberlain as a salesman or manager. From about 1806, for almost a century, Grainger were rivals of the main Worcester factories and, while their wares were generally cheaper and aimed at a less affluent market, at its best Grainger showed that they could manufacture products of as fine a quality as Chamberlain. The pair of hunting mugs shown on the cover of this guide were made by Grainger in about 1810 and are worthy of the high price (£7,260) paid for them in 1987.

BELOW *A cup and saucer of c.1835, marked only with a pattern number but exactly matching the Grainger factory pattern book.* Worcester Royal Porcelain Company.

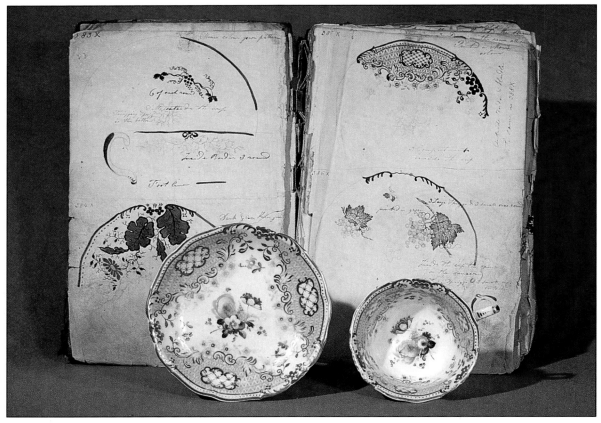

I have recently been involved in extensive research into the Grainger factory and have discovered, at first hand, the process of detective work necessary to identify the wares of many smaller English factories. Factory pattern books, shape books, and other records from Grainger survive at Worcester and these have identified many teaware shapes. In addition, my father, Henry Sandon, and I have rescued many thousands of discarded fragments unearthed by a new road passing through a corner of the Grainger factory site. These unfinished, broken pieces were damaged during manufacture at all different periods of the factory's existence; some correspond exactly with teaware shapes not previously attributed and, until now, masquerading as 'Staffordshire'. Archaeology is not restricted to eighteenth-century factory sites. Indeed, I have been involved in methodical excavations of several twentieth-century pottery sites to learn about the products made there. It is worrying to think that if we had not been interested and dedicated enough to watch the new road developments in Worcester, all of the vital information we have learnt from the unfinished Grainger fragments would have been lost forever. Many porcelain factory sites are known and can be visited by collectors. With permission, large or small scale excavations can be planned and archaeology can help fill many of the gaps in our

BELOW *The tray from a cabaret set of Swansea porcelain painted in the pretty style from France which was very popular, particularly in London during the 1810s. 30 cm (12 in); impressed Swansea mark.*

knowledge. Few archaeologists consider nineteenth-century sites old enough to be taken seriously, but I hope that in the not too distant future this attitude will change with respect to porcelain sites.

By the 1820s the hard outlines of the classical Greek styles had been replaced. There was a natural progression towards designs based on the art of Imperial Rome, as interpreted by the French Empire under Napoleon. The Empire style emerged as a reaction against the rococo shapes made before the Revolution in France. In addition, Napoleon's campaign in Egypt brought to the forefront in French art motifs of sphinxes, obelisks, and hawks. Handles of vases became eagles or caryatids – winged maidens – in burnished gold. Cup handles became serpents or the necks of swans, their wings engulfing the vessels. Brightly polished gold was used abundantly, contrasted with the unglazed white biscuit porcelain used for some of

BELOW RIGHT *Tasteful feather painting on a purely classical shape made by Flight of Worcester; c.1810, 8.5 cm (3¼ in) high.*

BELOW *Once again believed by its owner to be French, but this vase shape was unique to Swansea. In this case the painting is by Powell of Wimpole Street, London. 11 cm (4¼ in), c.1817.*

the handles. Panels bore fine paintings of classical subjects or a new range of subject matter, inspired by nature – flowers, animals or shells. In Paris, the new style was known as 'Empire' or 'Imperial'; in Germany, 'Biedermeier', to reflect its availability to all levels of society. English collectors use the tag 'French Empire', as well as the rather more wide-ranging 'Regency', to denote Britain's attempts at imitating the wares from Europe.

Named after the Prince Regent, whose taste was as flamboyant as it possibly could be, Regency-period English porcelain can vary from the rich 'Japan' patterns mentioned earlier, to very simple and subtle designs inspired by the more elegant porcelains imported from Paris – two styles which were worlds apart. No enterprise sums up overall taste in Britain during the Regency period better than the porcelains made at Swansea. William Billingsley's superb white china body was the nearest thing to French porcelain achieved in England, and his experiences at Derby and Worcester had given him a good insight into what the lucrative London market was looking for. Thomas Baxter, who moved to Swansea in 1816, had an even better idea of London taste, and together with other talented painters he and Billingsley produced some of the most elegant porcelain ever seen in this country.

FAR RIGHT *Recently identified as New Hall, this service is painted with illustrations of Dr. Syntax, c.1825. The decoration is unsophisticated and typical of a Staffordshire maker.*

At Swansea they made a small number of 'Japan' patterns and a variety of formal coloured border designs of a traditional style with the more florid versions undoubtedly copied directly from Paris porcelain. More subtle and delicate were flower patterns painted by Thomas Pardoe, David Evans and William Pollard in a style that became the hallmark of Welsh porcelain. Wild flowers, simply scattered or highly garlanded, were painted in soft colours against the whiteness of the porcelain. Evans was described as 'the best wild flower painter in the business' and his delicate pink, yellow and flesh tints have a refreshing lightness. Pollard, in contrast, used stronger outlines and autumnal tints, often including wild strawberries in his groupings. With gentle rather than overpowering gilding to finish off the designs, Swansea had created a style which was to remain popular until well after the demise of the factory itself.

Landscape painting at Swansea matched the quality of the flower work in its subtlety. The views painted there were not heavy and finely detailed, like John Penningtons's work at Worcester or that of the other artists who followed him. Instead, they owed more to the influence of Zachariah Boreman who had taught his style to Billingsley at Derby. The paintings are rarely restricted by the harsh confines of a square or round panel. Rather, they fade into the white porcelain with a soft outline similar to the 'picturesque' style practised principally at Derby. The picturesque style was a form of landscape painting whereby the main features of a view – trees, rocks, a cottage or a ruin – were re-arranged to make a more attractive compostion. The view was not taken from nature, but was instead an idealized version.

BELOW *A garniture of Chamberlain Worcester vases painted by Humphrey Chamberlain himself with Shakespearean scenes against a marbled background; 25 cm (10 in). Made c.1815, the vases are sheer extravagance.*

The style can be seen at its best in the work of Samuel Smith who replaced Baxter as the principal landscape artist at the Flight factory. Illustrated here, a garniture of Worcester vases by Smith, painted in about 1815, epitomize English Regency porcelain. The shapes are adapted from classical ideas inspired by Vienna or other continental porcelain, while the landscapes, although titled underneath, are purely imaginary, the main features re-arranged in the best picturesque traditions. Sold in 1980 for £1,760, they would have increased in value by three times that amount a decade later – such is the demand for the top quality porcelain of this period.

The painted panel had become the most important part of a piece of porcelain in this period. In complete contrast to the subtlety of Swansea porcelain, that of Worcester represented the height of extravagance. Theatrical scenes, luscious flowers, shells painted from nature, or groups of bird feathers – all were painted with a degree of realism never seen before, and a richness rarely seen again. Collecting Regency Worcester and Swansea procelain is virtually impossible nowadays owing to the high prices, but some of the finest pieces are in museum collections, and quality such as this is worth travelling across the country to see.

BELOW *Flight of Worcester, by 1810, was producing some of the finest porcelain ever made in this country. These vases, painted by Samuel Smith, are simply breathtaking; 27 cm (10½ in), full script marks.*

Chapter Ten

The Revival of Rococo

While the Regency era was represented by strong classical shapes and richly painted panels, the 1830s saw the arrival of a much more gentle, feminine style which stepped back nearly ninety years into the past. The rococo movement in the 1740s had represented a reaction against the hard symmetry and angles of the baroque. After half a century of classicism, punctuated with the occasional chinoiserie, British taste had sought novelty. A new feeling in English porcelain had begun in South Wales when Swansea looked to France for inspiration. Collectors had begun to acquire the *pâte tendre* of Sèvres from the 1760s and 1770s and vast sums were paid for services and vases with rich coloured grounds. George IV bought several major Sèvres services. His most important purchase in 1802 was secured with the help of Harry Phillips, the auctioneer and founder of the present firm. By private sale, the Duchess of Manchester sold the service which had been given to her by Louis XVI. The Prince Regent paid £840, a large sum in those days, even though Mr Phillips had managed to get the price reduced by £210. Instead of heavily painted panels, this service was decorated with fruit and flower sprays within a turquoise border; many similar designs in the more feminine Sèvres style were eagerly sought by collectors among the English gentry.

In 1817 William Billingsley transferred to Nantgarw, where his white porcelain plates almost all copied original Sèvres shapes. Most were decorated in London and the designs most favoured were coloured borders and pretty flower painting, the ground moulded with rococo scrolls and flowers. Some which were unmarked were probably sold to dealers as French porcelain. Others were treasured as Nantgarw porcelain in its own right, and many collectors feel, probably correctly, that Nantgarw is the most beautiful porcelain body manufactured in England.

Difficulty in firing this delicate china led to the downfall of the factory after only three years. Large numbers of white plates were sent to London, however, where the china dealers employed artists to decorate them in up-to-date French styles. Firms such as Robins and Randall and Powell of Wigmore Street sold London-decorated Nantgarw porcelain and found a ready market for the wares. The same dealers also sold Coalport and Minton porcelain and naturally they reported to these factories information as to what pieces were selling best in their London shops. When Billingsley himself turned up at Coalport in 1820, penniless and desperate for employment, John Rose, the proprietor, was more than glad to hire him on generous terms in order to fill the gap left by the demise of the Welsh factories using his own feldspar porcelain. This was not very different from Nantgarw and much easier and cheaper to make.

Although Coalport claimed to be the natural successor to Swansea and Nantgarw, even incorporating their names in its factory backstamp, there is no reason to suppose that it took over any of the Welsh factory's moulds. Billingsley had deserted his backers in Wales and left them with a useless stock of materials, but at Coalport there was no shortage of good moulds for making the same copies of old Sèvres shapes which had been supplied to the London trade for some time. The porcelain made at Coalport from 1820 can very easily be confused with Welsh wares, especially when it was painted in London by the same artists and gilders who decorated most of Nantgarw's wares. Only a few years after the closure of the Nantgarw works its fine porcelain became legendary. White stocks in London ran out and some of the dealers added the Nantgarw name to Coalport and even to French porcelain painted in London. The fine dessert service illustrated here is by a painter whose work is well known on Nantgarw. Here, though, the porcelain originates from Paris, painted in London and bearing no factory mark.

Nantgarw marked virtually every plate it made, and many other shapes, with its impressed stamp 'Nant-Garw C.W.', the C.W. standing for China Works. It never, however, used any form of written mark, so if the name Nantgarw is painted onto the bottom of a piece in either red or brown enamel, it will not be genuine. Other attributions are open to considerable question and are very difficult to authenticate. Coalport probably made cups and saucers which were identical to Welsh shapes, especially a range of teawares where the saucers had solid, flat, unglazed bases. These are regularly offered for sale in shops and auction rooms as Nantgarw, but great care has to be taken, as many experts now cast serious doubt on such attributions. Although the London decoration will be the same, the value of a Swansea or Nantgarw piece will be very, very much greater than that of its Coalport equivalent.

The most popular Sèvres shape, known in the eighteenth century as *assiette à palmes*, was adapted by English and Welsh

ABOVE *Part of an extensive Ridgway service of 1825-1830, the quality of the flower painting matched only by the fine gilded borders in neo-rococo style.*

factories. Versions of this shape were made at Worcester, Coalport, Derby, Davenport, and many other factories, most bearing no mark of any sort. Any example which cannot be called Welsh is usually labelled Coalport, but often this attribution is itself questionable. Without a factory mark it is virtually impossible to identify a maker with any certainty, and the quality of many services is vastly inferior to Coalport. The shape of plate could be decorated in a great many ways. I remember visiting a grand country house to carry out a valuation of the porcelain, and was asked particularly about the Coalport dessert set. I had to admit that I could not find one, just a lot of odd plates stacked in a cupboard. 'That's it!', I was told, 'it's a harlequin set'; and indeed it was. Every plate, and there were twenty-three of them, was of the same *assiette à palmes* shape, but each was decorated in a totally different way – flowers, landscapes, birds, some with coloured borders, some without. The dozen or so dishes which accompanied the plates were all totally different again, united only by the moulded border design. Harlequin services were popular in the early-nineteenth century. They served to impress as well as entertain, as each course was served on a different pattern and guests

would debate with their neighbours over dinner as to who had the richest or nicest patterns on their plate. Most harlequin sets have been split up now as their owners did not realize that they belonged together. It would be possible, however, to put such a set back together by acquiring a particular shape of dessert plate in English porcelain, regardless of the decoration. This is an interesting and original way to collect.

Times were changing in England and towards the 1830s taste became much more extravagant. Customers called for more ornament and looked towards the excesses of the eighteenth-century rococo. Sèvres was tame in comparison with the richest Chelsea of the 'Gold Anchor' period, and some factories made direct copies of Chelsea 'silver shape' dishes, plates, and vases which had been originally modelled eighty years before. The neo-rococo age had truly begun, and symmetrical shapes were now considered old-fashioned. Everyone wanted sweeping curves and shell-like scrolls, with as much of the new decoration as could conceivably be incorporated into a single piece of porcelain. Every space would be filled with a painted panel, scroll surround, or coloured ground with intricate rims and handles; the shape and the decoration vying to present the most ornate effect.

All factories moved into this period with richer patterns and shapes, but the two makers probably most influenced by the neo-rococo were Coalport and Rockingham. Their wares were essentially similar, but whereas the former was slick and sophisticated, the latter was extraordinarily rustic and eccentric.

Coalports's rococo revival is best illustrated by the class of ware it called 'Coalbrookdale', a most unsuitable name associated with

ABOVE *Three 'Coalbrookdale' vases from the Coalport factory, the most flamboyant rococo shapes imaginable in delicate colours and rich gold; 47 cm (18½ in), 1830-1835.*

BELOW *A massive Coalport vase using the leaf and scroll designs of the neo-rococo to rather better effect than many pieces made in this style, particularly at Rockingham. 44 cm (17½ in) high, c.1835.*

ABOVE *A range of Rockingham wares typical of the popular styles of the 1830s. The pelican handled vase is bizarre with its green and gold striped neck adding to the curious effect.*

heavy cast-iron work made locally. Coalbrookdale porcelain was moulded with scrollwork heightened in delicate coloured enamels and gold and, in additon to painted flowers, it was further ornamented with realistically modelled and coloured flowers. The porcelain blossoms, individually made and stuck on, produced a very decorative and pretty ornament that brought a touch of the countryside to the drawing rooms of city houses.

Flowers featured prominently in painted decoration on Coalport and Rockingham teawares; pretty coloured sprays were contained within very elaborate border patterns. Frequently, two contrasting or complimentary ground colours combined with gilding to form a fussy border decoration which tended to confuse the overall effect. Elaborate handle shapes and moulded rims further complicated the designs, resulting in a style quite unlike the elegant Regency. At their best, with single colour grounds and sympathetic gold edging, the 1830s designs can be attractive and perfectly suited to modern tastes. Unfortunately, intricate gilding and fine painting used on the much busier patterns are so confused that the quality cannot be appreciated, the eye being dazzled by too much ornament. On a large vase, or even on a plate or dish, there is enough room for busy decoration to work. But, it was the smaller pieces which tended to suffer most from over-decoration.

The result of the busy, confused designs was that the tea sets of the 1830s and 1840s were much more likely to have been split up by past owners who could not hope to find a buyer for a complete service.

Single cups and saucers will be worth less than more classic designs of a few years earlier, even though they were more expensive when they were made. Though they are less popular today, it must be remembered that in the 1830s the public very much wanted these busy patterns. Every factory in Staffordshire made them, as well as the provincial factories of Coalport and Rockingham. In Worcester, Grainger and Chamberlain moved with the times and produced hundreds of different intricate designs, each fancy border available in a variety of colour combinations. Flight's factory never made the changeover. Their failure to supply the new styles that the public wanted led to the decline of the factory and, facing virtual

bankruptcy, they were forced to amalgamate with their rivals, Chamberlain, in 1840.

There was much competition between factories to produce neo-rococo tea services, and china dealers could stock the wares of a considerable number of different makers. As had occurred earlier in the century, to protect their own trade the retailers did not want their customers to know the name of the actual manufacturer. Customers would have to return to the shop if they wanted to re-order pieces because the retailers had encouraged the makers to omit their names from their services. Most china dating from this period is marked only with a pattern number. Until modern research had identified many of the smaller factories, it was possible to give an attribution to only a very few of these tea services.

One exception was the Rockingham porcelain factory, established by the Brameld family on the estate of Earl Fitzwilliam, the Marquess of Rockingham, at Swinton in Yorkshire. Originally making earthenwares, porcelain came into production in around 1825, and by 1830 the factory was a major producer of porcelain teawares. Similar in style to contemporary products of Coalport and Staffordshire, the principal difference lay in the fact that Rockingham marked almost every saucer in its services with the factory mark of a griffin, derived from the arms of Earl Fitzwilliam.

By the early 1900s, when collectors began to research nineteenth-century porcelain, the Rockingham mark had become very well known. It was associated with the kinds of services the

ABOVE *One of a pair of spill holders which shows that not all Rockingham's vase shapes are eccentric, although the picturesque landscapes are rich and imaginary; 12.5 cm (5 in), griffin mark, c.1830.*

ABOVE LEFT *A group of Staffordshire porcelain ornaments, 1830-1860, all of types still frequently referred to as Rockingham. Sadly nothing like any of these was made at Rockingham.*

factory was producing, and because similar services by all the other makers were unmarked, the same collectors assumed that all had been made at Rockingham. This misunderstanding has been perpetuated and even today a great many Staffordshire, Coalport, or Worcester tea sets are called, by family tradition, 'Rockingham' because of their similarity to griffin-marked pieces. In truth, only a tiny proportion of all pieces called 'Rockingham' were actually made at the Yorkshire factory, and, of these, the majority will be marked on the saucers of the sets.

Even without marks, the wares made at Rockingham are distinctive. Their modellers favoured a particularly rustic interpretation of the rococo and, with the exception of one popular shape made at every factory, all of their cup forms were unique to the factory. They ranged from handles with sharp spurs on top to a remarkable cup modelled with primrose leaves and gnarled twigs forming the handle. Teapots were particularly flamboyant including one with a knob in the form of a crown.

Ornamental wares reflected the rusticity to an even greater extent. Twisting branches, primrose leaves and scrollwork appear everywhere, heightened with colours and gold, and painted with flower sprays. Eccentric is a word which sums up many of the Rockingham forms and, while strange and curiously beautiful in their own way, they are really something of an acquired taste. The spill vases with heavily picturesque landscapes are unusually tame for Rockingham and rather more successful than most of their products.

Rockingham made flower-encrusted porcelain – mostly as scent bottles – as well as a range of minature teapots and cabinet pieces. Similar to the Coalbrookdale china, but more rustic, the Rockingham examples are generally much more expensive today because the factory has acquired an almost cult following. There is no doubt that some pieces are very tasteful, but to appreciate fully the extreme of Rockingham, the collector must visit the Victoria and Albert Museum in London or the Rotherham Museum in Yorkshire to see the two rhinoceros vases. Unbelievably ornate creations and more than 1m high (3 feet), it is impossible to describe them; they have to be seen to be believed, representing the triumph of technical advancement over good taste.

Rockingham made a wide range of figures and animal models; fortunately most are marked either with an impressed griffin or else a red-painted class number unique to the factory. Many copy Derby, while others resemble subjects made by many small porcelain factories in Staffordshire. A number were ornamented with fine shredded clay, pushed through a sieve and applied to the model to simulate vegetation. Once again, confusion arose because, while Rockingham models were usually marked, none of the other Staffordshire makers ever put their name on their products. Just as collectors assumed all 1830s tea services were made at Rockingham, they similarly assumed that any simple figure or animal model in porcelain with shredded clay details was also made there. Two types of ornament became particularly associated with the name

LEFT *A Derby model of a fox, a Charles Bourne ram, and a pair of unidentified hedgehogs. The range of animals made in English porcelain seems limitless and a lively collection can be formed.*

Rockingham though without any evidence whatsoever to support such an attribution; these are represented on page 105.

The white woolly coats of sheep and poodles were ideally represented by shredded clay. Inexpensive novelties, these dog and sheep models were tremendously popular during the 1830s and 1840s and examples by a variety of makers, including Chamberlain and Grainger in Worcester, can be collected. Most, however, were made by small Staffordshire firms and cannot be identified. One point worth noting, though, is that none were actually made at the Rockingham factory.

A great many other sorts of animals were made by the Staffordshire factories, in particular dogs and cats, but also exotic species such as leopards and elephants, giraffes and even hedgehogs. Rarely more than 7 cm-10 cm long (3-4 inches), these porcelain models can form a most charming collection, although they are becoming more expensive all the time. Simple sheep or poodles are reasonably cheap, while rare animals or examples from Derby or Worcester fetch much higher prices. Staffordshire models are mostly unmarked, although certain rare sheep were made by Charles Bourne's factory and a very wide range were made by Samuel Alcock's factory, marked with an impressed model number on the underside of their bases, together with a tiny workman's mark. The attribution is based on fragments with similar markings found in a hidden cache of porcelain deposited by Alcock in the foundations of a building. Most examples are marked in this way and Alcock models should therefore be easily identifiable, although they rarely are.

The other kind of wares incorrectly associated with Rockingham are models of houses and cottages such as the group illustrated over. Examples made in porcelain are frequently encrusted with sieved clay vegetation – hence they are mistakenly

ABOVE *A selection of pastille burners in the form of rustic country cottages, including an example with a lilac ground, 1830-1845.*

labelled in the same way as the poodles and sheep. There is little doubt that Rockingham never made any such cottage models, although the factory's name has continued to be applied to them for a very long time.

The cottages were mostly made as pastille burners, essential items in every town house in the early-Victorian period. Their purpose was slowly to burn sweet smelling pastilles, the scented smoke drifting through the open chimneys and window. The general level of sanitation in cities such as London had improved little since Elizabethan days, with sewage flowing in open drains into the River Thames. At times the smell was unbearable and a pastille burner in every room was the only way to overcome the stench. Early examples were of plain conical shape, but by 1830 the 'cottage orne' had become the standard form. A rustic farm-house or gothic castle and, in particular, a tumbledown cottage served to remind city dwellers of the much more pleasant air of the countryside.

George Cruikshank, the caricaturist, produced a series of prints in the 1830s illustrating the effects of 'The Bottle'. One print shows a respectable family at home, with a typical cottage sitting on the mantelpiece between a pair of china dogs. Gradually, as the family is destroyed by the evils of strong drink, the cottage is no longer used as a pastille burner, but instead, clay tobacco pipes are kept in its chimneys.

The more expensive cottages have a separate tray in which to put the pastille, while cheaper ones have just an opening in the rear. Gradually, as sanitation improved, the cottages were no longer needed, and late-nineteenth century examples made from earlier moulds will have the openings at the back filled in. Other sorts, particularly castles, have open turrets or towers which were used to keep rolled up paper spills on a mantelpiece, to use as firelighters or to light pipes. Many were purely ornamental, to remind the owners of the countryside while serving no useful purpose at all.

Ten years ago Phillips sold a fine collection of one hundred and fifty models, including examples made by Coalport, Spode and

Chamberlain who made some of the best of all. More unusual novelties were formed as a church, a lighthouse, and a Georgian town house. They sold for up to £550 each for the best examples, and ten years later they have increased in value substantially. The simplest sort are still available at low prices. A reasonable collection can be formed, especially if you do not mind a little bit of damage. However, care must be taken when buying, as reproductions are fairly common. Some of the most sought-after pastille burners are in porcelain which has been stained a pale lilac colour; beware, these are frequently copied. If you are able to collect a number of cottages, they will give a great deal of pleasure, and nothing sums up more clearly the taste of the neo-rococo in English porcelain.

ABOVE *The Derby factory had generally declined by the 1830s, yet this vase of modelled flowers is unbelievably fine. Perfume would have been sprinkled on the flowers to combat the smells of the cities. 20 cm (8 in), marked Bloor Derby.*

LEFT *A pair of Minton candlesticks, 23 cm (9 in), c.1835. Inspired by Meissen of the same period, although the flower modelling is distinctively English.*

Chapter Eleven

High-Victorian Art and the Great Exhibition

The 1840s saw some significant changes in the English porcelain industry and in British art in general. The fancy styles were more in demand than ever, mainly because they appealed to the new kind of buyer who had emerged over the previous decade. The old aristocracy, whom the factories in Worcester and Derby had always relied on, had been replaced in the forefront of art patronage by the new commercial classes – the factory owners, industrialists and ship owners – who were anxious to spend their newly-acquired fortunes.

This new moneyed class wished to impress its wealth upon the environment and commissioned architects to build in the fashionable gothic style. Cathedral-like homes were to house art collections which looked like good value for money in that paintings were large and very detailed, with ornament playing a prominent role. The over-ornate porcelain services which Staffordshire and Coalport produced in vast quantities suited the taste of this new class; the market for rich, aristocratic pieces fell by the wayside. The reputations which Derby and Flight of Worcester had built up meant little to the industrialists and merchants. They wanted ostentation – but only at a certain price – and Staffordshire goods, while not so fine as Derby or Flight, were flashy enough and much cheaper. In 1830 the Derby factory, which had been struggling for some time under the contol of the Bloor family, finally closed for good. Meanwhile, there was insufficient patronage to support two great Worcester factories; in 1840 Flight and Chamberlain were forced to merge. The new partnership of Chamberlain & Co. fought hard to retain its place as a market leader, but could not compete with the bigger factories in Staffordshire. Ten years later, it too went bankrupt.

Public taste in the 1840s was frequently criticized. The *Daily Telegraph* at the time described it as 'of the coarsest and most uncouth order'. Certainly, at its most extreme, it was pretty appalling. Chamberlain, for example, made a model of King John's tomb in Worcester Cathedral, shown on page 118. As a subject this was rather tasteless, and made more so by the fact that inside the monument, instead of the poor king, was an inkwell, pounce pot and pen tray. Not everything made in England at this time was unrefined or without certain qualities, but many people felt that a great deal could be learnt from European manufacturers. Most prominent amongst the campaigners for an improvement in art in Britain were Prince Albert, the Prince Consort, and Henry Cole, an assistant Keeper at the Public Records Office. Both viewed the notion of a major exhibition of the Arts and Sciences as a chance for British manufacturers to show just what they were capable of alongside the best from all over the world, and also as an opportunity for the manufacturers to gain new inspiration from foreign competitors and from each other.

The result of the efforts of Prince Albert and Henry Cole is history. The great glass palace in Hyde Park was opened by the Queen on 1 May 1851. In the following five months over six million people visited the exhibition to marvel at the gothic folly of the medieval court, the Indian temples, and Chinese pagodas. Fantastic machines stood silent alongside their products from across Europe – metalwork from Germany, glass from France, and porcelain from England, Europe and the Far East.

All of the principal factories in Britain took stands at the exhibition, and the catalogue produced at the time is an invaluable directory of the products from all levels of manufacture of the time. The ceramics industry, in particular, was well represented. One theme ran throughout the exhibits submitted by the porcelain makers – a tendency towards over-decoration, often taken to extremes. The relative position of the different factories is shown by the standard of display they presented. Chamberlain & Co. of Worcester could only exhibit some fine works from the past and a range of pierced porcelain directly copied from contemporary Sèvres.

ABOVE *A pair of Chamberlain vases, 36 cm (14 in) high, c.1845, although in an earlier classical style. Certain styles remained popular over a long period and in this case it is easy to understand why.*

RIGHT *A pair of Coalport 'Chinese' vases made in 1840 in an eccentric combination of chinoiserie and rococo; 36 cm (14 in) high. Superb quality, if somewhat exaggerated.*

ABOVE *A Minton vase copying early Sèvres with a* rose Pompedour *ground; 50 cm (19½ in) high. The panel by Louis Jahn is typical of the work of European artists employed by the factory during the 1850s and 1860s.*

On the other hand, Coalport and Minton were able to display a fabulous range of new and exciting wares which put Worcester to shame. Both showed large vases in early-French styles, finely painted and richly gilded with strongly coloured grounds. Other pieces had modelled figures and cherubs supporting the bases or attached casually to the handles. Perhaps the biggest novelty at the Great Exhibition, in regard to ceramics, was a new form of porcelain, called 'parian'.

Copeland, the successor to the Spode factory, and Minton both claimed to have invented this new material, also known as 'statuary porcelain'. Parian was named after the Greek island of Paros, where some of the finest marble used by ancient sculptors was mined. It was, quite simply, an attempt to reproduce fine marble statues in a less expensive material. Henry Cole was a great supporter of parian and worked closely with Herbert Minton to promote it. The new formula meant that an original work of art, beyond the price range of most people, could be exactly copied so that anyone could own one. Critics argued that it debased the qualities of the original piece to have copies on sale in every china shop, but most sculptors themselves were fully in favour of parian.

Figures in unglazed white biscuit porcelain had been made since the eighteenth century. The difference between these and parian was the high glass content of the parian body which meant that the material need not be glazed to keep it clean. Parian figures could be placed amongst the clutter of a Victorian parlour and bring fine art to ordinary middle class homes. The popularity of the new ware was increased by clever marketing which Copeland, in particular, relied on. Two societies were formed to promote the works of artists. The Art Union of London and the Crystal Palace Art

LEFT *Three centrepieces from a Minton
dessert service, 26 cm (10¼ in) high overall,
dated 1861 and 1862, in parian body. Items
such as this would have been shown at many
international exhibitions.*

ABOVE *Royal Worcester employed Sir
Thomas Brock to model one of their most
popular figures: 'The Bather Surprised',
introduced in 1876. The blatant eroticism
was excused in the name of art and such
figures graced many respectable Victorian
homes. 26 cm (10¼ in).*

Union ran a form of art lottery whereby the lucky winners were
awarded prints or books. A number of well known artists were
commissioned to model sculptures which were then reduced in size
by means of a machine patented by Benjamin Cheverton. This
enabled a popular model to be copied in a number of different sizes,
and certain popular models were, quite literally, mass-produced.
'Clytie', probably the most popular of all, shows the head of a maiden
rising from an open flower. At least half a dozen makers produced
versions in several different sizes and, although introduced in the
1850s, the figure was still being produced seventy years later.

Charles Eastlake, a keen supporter of the gothic style,
illustrated in one of his works Clytie on a wooden bracket he had
designed himself. His *Hints on Household Taste* became a best-seller
guide to interior decoration. Parian figures and busts were ideally
suited to high-Victorian taste, and the new sculpture gallery in South
Kensington, set up with the profits from the Great Exhibition,
displayed casts of every famous statue from antiquity. Few were
copied exactly in parian. Instead, leading sculptors of the day
produced new studies, more suited to the sentimental themes of
Victorian life. Minton found a small gold mine in the work of John
Bell, who time and again was able to combine elegant modelling with
exactly the right amount of sentiment. His figures of Miranda and
Dorothea – judging by the numbers which still survive and we sell at
Phillips each year – must have graced almost every middle class
home in the 1860s. Though displaying a slight eroticism in the young
ladies' states of undress, they were acceptable because they were
considered 'art' and could therefore be displayed openly in an
otherwise stuffy home interior. My favourite is 'The Octaroon', a
naked adolescent girl, her hands bound by porcelain chains. It

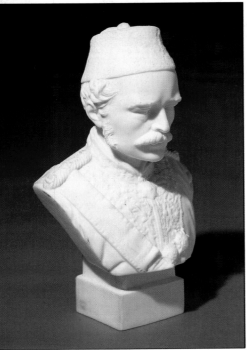

appears daring, even by today's standards, and must have caused quite a stir in Victorian society.

In 1984, an exhibition of parian ware was put on in Chelsea by the London dealer, Richard Dennis. The hundreds of figures were shown as they would originally have been displayed in one of the great Victorian exhibitions, crowded together on giant pyramids and producing an effect which I will never forget. As decoration, in a complementary setting, parian can be displayed very successfully in a modern home, but for every admirer of the tasteful white sculptural porcelain, there are several who find it ghost-like, funereal and particularly dull. Lack of colour does make it a very specialized taste which, for a long time, was largely ignored by collectors. Revived interest in the Victorian period in the 1960s, and the publication by Shinn of the standard reference work on the subject, caused collectors to think again and prices rose significantly. Many people predicted further rises, but over the last decade there has been very little real change, mostly because of the impracticality of collecting large parian figures. The exhibition of 1984 certainly helped, and prices have risen again. 'The Veiled Bride' by Rafaelle Monti is Copeland's best known and finest study. The girl's face, revealed through the veil, is produced by a single casting and shows remarkable skill on the part of the modeller. Not everybody would want one, but the workmanship is admirable. The example illustrated here sold in 1988 for £1,045, which, in fact, represented a fall in price from two or three years earlier. Thus it is difficult to predict that parian will have much investment potential in the foreseeable future, but as a mirror of Victorian taste, a modest collection of parian is well worth considering. Robinson and Leadbeater's popular series of small busts – such as that of General Gordon illustrated here – can still be bought cheaply.

Worcester's failure to exhibit parian at the Great Exhibition showed how far they had fallen behind their rivals. The factory needed new blood and the fresh impetus came with the arrival of two new directors, W. H. Kerr and Richard William Binns. The new company, known as Kerr & Binns, wasted no time in introducing a high quality parian. They had many Irish contacts and wanted to make an impressive display at the forthcoming Dublin Exhibition of 1853. As a centrepiece, they decided to make a dessert service based on Shakespeare's *A Midsummer Night's Dream*. It was modelled by a young Irish sculptor, William Boyton Kirk, and combined parian statuary with very richly painted and gilded porcelain.

A selection of pieces from this Shakespeare service was sold at Phillips in 1984 and are illustrated opposite. This service had been greatly admired when Queen Victoria visited the Dublin Exhibition, and led to R. W. Binns receiving an invitation to visit Buckingham Palace with a range of Worcester's latest products. Prince Albert had a keen fondness for porcelain, with a particular interest in copies of Limoges enamel; he encouraged the Worcester artists to try these on different background colours.

With the 'Medieval Court' at the Crystal Palace and the renewed interest in the gothic styles, Limoges enamel of the sixteenth

and seventeenth centuries enjoyed a considerable revival. Minton made copies in porcelain of the Limoges styles, but it was Kerr & Binns who led the field with the work of Thomas Bott. The Limoges technique involved building up a design with layer upon layer of white enamel on top of a strongly coloured background. Instead of the black ground of Limoges, Bott preferred the deep royal blue which Worcester had perfected since the eighteenth century. Bott's work was unbelievably fine and, although he is best known for the service ordered by Queen Victoria on a turquoise ground, the deep blue Limoges enamels Worcester exhibited in France in 1856 were worthy of the high praise heaped upon him at the time.

Bott's skills improved steadily and in 1866 he began his finest creations, a pair of vases and a ewer commemorating the eight hundredth anniversary of the Norman Conquest. Copied from Daniel Maclise's prints published by the Art Union of London, the three pieces took Bott two whole years to complete, so painstakingly slow was the Limoges technique. A selection of pieces left unfinished

ABOVE *A selection of pieces from the 'Shakespeare Service' in parian and glazed porcelain, made by Kerr & Binns of Worcester for the Dublin Exhibition of 1853. The models by William Boyton Kirk were much admired by Queen Victoria.*

FAR LEFT ABOVE *A Copeland bust of 'The Veiled Bride' modelled originally by Rafaelle Monti. His marble sculpture was superbly reproduced in parian and highly acclaimed in its day. 38 cm (15 in), c.1860.*

FAR LEFT BELOW *General Gordon, the Hero of Khartoum, modelled in parian by Robinson and Leadbetter, 15 cm (6 in), c.1885. The factory made busts of virtually every popular Victorian personality and examples are generally inexpensive today.*

RIGHT *A tazza in Limoges enamel style by Thomas Bott Snr. made by Kerr & Binns. The rich blue ground sets the figures off superbly. 25 cm (10 in), c.1860.*

BELOW *A monumental vase, 66 cm (26 in), modelled and decorated by Antonin Boullemier for the Staffordshire firm of Brown-Westhead, Moore & Co., c.1885. High-Victorian art has been taken to extremes, although in this case the effect is relatively pleasing.*

by his untimely death in 1870 is preserved at the Dyson Perrins Museum in Worcester, where many of his finest creations can be seen. Bott's son, Thomas John Bott, also excelled in the Limoges technique. Trained at the Royal Worcester Factory by his father, he left the factory to work on his own, and plaques such as that shown opposite were enamelled in his own kiln on blue-glazed blanks supplied from Staffordshire. Skilled in many branches of porcelain production, T. J. Bott subsequently became art director of the Coalport factory.

Examples of Worcester Limoges enamel rarely appear on the market, but when they do they are, I feel, very undervalued considering the work involved. Because they took so long to decorate, they were very expensive in the 1860s and 1870s, and in real terms they are worth less today than they would have cost new.

A new trend had been set by the parian sculptures and Limoges enamels. Instead of being produced anonymously, the new-style pieces were marketed by the factories as the works of specific artists, such as John Bell and Thomas Bott. Generally, porcelain factories did not permit their workmen to sign their names on their work, perhaps out of a fear of losing artists to rival firms, or else because it might give the craftsmen an inflated idea of their worth and lead them to demand more money. By the 1860s, however, factories like Minton, Worcester and Wedgwood realized that there were advantages in allowing top painters to sign their work. Collectors would be eager to build up collections of signed pieces, either by one particular artist or by a variety. The French porcelain industry had fallen on hard times, and many leading craftsmen from Paris and Sèvres came to England in search of employment. Minton, in particular, saw the potential of these artists and offered them generous terms to join the factory or to paint in their own studios, on a sort of freelance basis.

Virtually all of the most important decorators working in England in the 1860s and 1870s were Frenchmen. Minton employed Léon Arnoux, Edward Rischglitz, Antonin and Lucien Boullemier, and Emile Lessore (who also worked for Wedgwood) – artists all highly skilled in styles that diverged greatly from the Staffordshire traditions. At Worcester, Edward Bejot became a principal designer responsible for the introduction of many French styles. Both Bejot and Lessore preferred to spend most of their time in Paris, and it was worthwhile for Worcester and Wedgwood to send partly finished wares over to Paris for decorating in these artists' own studios.

While all highly-regarded in their day, only a few of the French artists have maintained their popularity, and pieces by some of the lesser-known names can be bought at quite reasonable prices. Lucien Bèsche, a Frenchman who worked for Copeland and other English factories, was represented by two signed dishes sold at Phillips in 1987 and 1988. In delicate French styles which, perhaps, are rather alien to English taste, they sold for less than £100 each, and were in my view extremely cheap, especially when compared with Emile Lessore, whose work fetches four or five times as much because his name is better known.

It is not surprising that the French artists brought contemporary French styles with them, and while the market for these was good in the 1860s, there was a greater demand for the more traditional French wares. Minton specialized in exact reproductions of virtually every eighteenth-century Sèvres vase shape, copied from original specimens lent by wealthy collectors. Antonin Boullemier painted many of the panels with sentimental and sweet little boys and cherubs, while nymphs and satyrs cavorted on larger panels or in the centres of dessert services. The ornate shapes and background colours showed some signs of becoming less overpowering in the 1870s, allowing the paintings to stand up for themselves. However, many very elaborately decorated wares were still being made, with worse examples to come. The best products of Minton and Copeland and, to a lesser extent, Worcester, made in the Sèvres style in the 1870s can be very beautiful and are often quite stunning. Vases – such as the fine example illustrated on page 118 – are understandably expensive, fitting easily into most modern decorative interiors.

One Frenchman I have neglected to mention had such a profound influence on the history of English porcelain that he almost deserves a chapter to himself. Not only was Marc Louis Solon a major artist, but as a collector and writer, he pioneered much of the original research into early English ceramics. His love for the rustic crudeness of early pottery was in complete contrast to the decoration he gave to his own pots – a style which was quite unmistakable.

While working for the Sèvres factory, Solon mastered the

ABOVE *'The Source'; a plaque in Limoges enamel style decorated in Worcester by Thomas John Bott, Jr. who achieved amazing detail by building up layers of enamel. 25 cm (10 in), dated 1883.*

RIGHT *The popularity of gothic styles in the 1840s led to some astonishing creations. This Chamberlain model of King John's Tomb in Worcester Cathedral opens to reveal an inkstand; 20 cm (8 in), c.1850.*

BELOW *A Minton vase decorated in* pâte-sur-pâte *by Marc Louis Solon, the greatest exponent of the technique; 35 cm (14 in). The eroticism of this example is fairly tame compared with some of his work.*

technique of *pâte-sur-pâte*, quite literally paste on paste. This was a process which gave a finished product not unlike, and often confused with, the Limoges enamel wares. Instead of building up layers of enamel fired over the glaze, Solon worked in coloured clay. Onto a dark background, he painted layers of white clay which could be modelled and carved rather like a shell cameo. When the correct thickness and detail had been achieved, the design was permanently sealed beneath a clear glaze, and as long as the glaze was properly controlled, none of the fine detail was hidden.

In France, Solon signed his work with his initials, M.L.S., or with the pseudonym 'Miles'. At Minton, where he moved in 1870, he preferred to use 'L. Solon', his neat signature appearing on every piece he made. Solon usually used white for his figures, while the background colours varied enormously, although there was a slight preference for a slatey blue-grey colour, with perhaps a tint of green or brown. These backgrounds were much more muddy and less violent than the deep blue of Bott's Limoges enamels. Borders were painted in a limited range of other colours and gilding contrasted dramatically with the ground colours.

Pâte-sur-pâte was not exclusive to Minton, but other factories made examples so far behind in terms of quality that they do not really count. From small posy holders to the largest exhibition vases standing more than 1.2 cm (4 feet) high, one characteristic of Solon's work remains constant – he never produced an inferior piece. His output was vast: mostly made up of rectangular plaques and pairs of vases, of which the example shown here is typical. The acrobatic nymph displays, through the thinness of her costumes, the eroticism which seems to underlie most of Solon's work. His near-naked maidens are often bound in chains or suffer varying fortunes at the hands of Cupid and his attendant *putti*; whips and chains are often featured and, at their most extreme, these designs reflect what must have been the very disturbed mind of a genius.

Large pairs of vases by Solon will sell for thousands of pounds, and any small vase or plaque will now fetch a sum well into four figures. Other *pâte-sur-pâte* can be less expensive, although all signed work is sought-after. The popularity of Minton's *pâte-sur-pâte* meant that other artists had to be taught the technique. Much influenced by Solon, the work of Albione Birks is regarded by some as almost equal to that of the master himself – a claim I feel is unjustified, even though Birks at his best can be very fine. In a more formal style, Charles Toft produced magnificent geometric designs in multi-coloured *pâte-sur-pâte* for Minton.

Edward Locke and William Pointon used the technique at Worcester, while Frederick Schenk developed his own particular style of *pâte-sur-pâte* for the smaller Staffordshire factory of George Jones. Nymphs and birds in tropical foliage appear on circular plaques, vases and wall-pockets, often signed 'F. Schenk', and resembling Minton, though coarser. It struck me, however, after we sold at Phillips exactly the same plaque as two other London salerooms in the same year, that these pieces were not all that they

LEFT *A direct copy of an early Sèvres* vaisseau à mat *vase made by Kerr &* Binns, *c.1855. 45 cm (17¾ in) high.*

BELOW RIGHT *Minton pâte-sur-pâte vases by A. Morgan, the simple styles and charming subject making this a most attractive pair. 15 cm (6 in), c.1875.*

BELOW A *pâte-sur-pâte* plaque *by Frederick Schenk made at George Jones' factory. Close examination reveals the design to be moulded. 30.3 cm (12 in).*

ABOVE *A Landseer painting copied faithfully onto a Royal Worcester plaque by James Bradley, 40 cm (16 in), dated 1874. Customers could commission copies of any painting they liked, painted in rich ceramic colours.*

FAR RIGHT *Charles Toft was a very influential artist in mid-Victorian English ceramics. He decorated this* pâte-sur-pâte *tour de force for Minton in 1878; 58 cm (23 in) high.*

seemed. Schenk had developed a method of moulding the design, painting the white clay into the mould and then pouring the dark clay ground in around it. If you look closely, there is the odd leaf which the white clay has not filled, leaving the detail in the background colour instead of picked out in white. Care has to be taken, as some Minton plates and cups and saucers were decorated with *pâte-sur-pâte* panels signed by A. Birks, but moulded in the same way as the George Jones pieces. The biggest giveaway is when there is a set of plates and two or more have identical panels, proving that they could not have been modelled by hand. It is very difficult to convince anyone that these Minton plates are not, in fact, fine original *pâte-sur-pâte*.

Fortunately, there is no real substitute for quality, and once the main English factories had regained their positions as producers of the finest porcelain, convincing fakes were just not practicable. The quality of painting and gilding on the expensive wares from the first division factories cannot be reproduced except by equally skilled painters with years of training behind them. If you could afford to pay for it you could have any painting you chose in the centre of a plate; Worcester and Minton regularly supplied to order direct copies of the best-selling artists of the day. If you did not own an original 'Stag at Bay' by Sir Edwin Landseer, Robert Perling would paint one for you on a Worcester plate. Joseph Williams could copy any painting by Miles Birket Foster or Thomas Sydney Cooper, and even the great J.M.W. Turner could be converted to china colours on a plate or dish. Turner's painting, 'Bacchus and Ariadne', appeared on a plate sold at Phillips in 1988. It was painted by Joseph Williams in the 1880s, and sold for £550, once again a reasonable price for such quality. Some fine Victorian porcelain is now very expensive, but many wonderful art works can still be collected at much more affordable prices.

Chapter Twelve
Japanesque and Late-Victorian Splendour

The popularity of parian brought about a new interest in figure-making in England. The parian body, even when glazed, could be modelled and fired much more delicately than previous bone china figures, and other skills had greatly improved since the days of Derby figure-making twenty years earlier. Factories developed new techniques and looked to continental styles for their models. Minton and Wedgwood used coloured majolica glazes on their earthenware bodies, and the Sèvres influence led Minton to try out all-over bright turquoise enamel on porcelain figures of *putti*, the bases highlighted in gold. Worcester also used bright turquoise glazes combined with matt red and brown. But, the effect was far from admired at the time. Much more successful was their glazed parian body which had a creamy finish capable of taking delicate enamel colours and gold.

R. W. Binns, the director at Worcester, greatly admired Italian art and set out to copy the figurines and embossed wares made at Naples at the end of the eighteenth century. The factory reproduced what they believed incorrectly to be 'Capo di Monte' figures, and marketed them under this name or under the name 'Raphaelesque', an equally inappropriate title since the style bore no relation to the paintings of Raphael at all. The figures reflected typical Victorian sentiment, chubby-cheeked *putti* playing cymbals and tambourines and maidens in diaphanous robes holding water pots, the pastel colouring producing a much prettier effect than parian ware.

The success of these figures set the course of the factory for the

rest of the century. Worcester was to become the most important figure-maker as a fashion for coloured models replaced the market for parian during the 1870s and 1880s. The factory's success as figure-makers was due almost entirely to one man: James Hadley, probably the finest English modeller of all time. Hadley was a local craftsman who had received little formal training, and yet he was able to design and model in any style the market wanted. Vases, teawares, and figures in classical, Middle Eastern, Chinese or rustic English – he attempted them all and his work was always perfectly executed.

The skill needed to model a complicated large vase was as great as that for any figure group, and yet Hadley is rarely given credit for this. Instead, he is famous for his figures of children, London characters, and Eastern water carriers, their faces modelled with tremendous strength, their costumes vigorous and without the complicated detail which would have made moulding difficult. His finest work, in my view, was amongst his smallest figures – a set of six characters down on their luck and forced to walk the streets of London carrying sandwich boards. The advertising boards were made of cardboard, on which a menu was written as the figures were placed around a dinner table – an idea reverting back to the use of figures for an eighteenth-century dessert course. A toff, a Chinaman, an old soldier of the Crimean War – the sort of people who lived in London's East End in the 1870s, all were modelled with pathos and understanding. Single figures of children inspired by the popular

FAR LEFT *'The French Fisherman', a Royal Worcester figure showing the superb modelling skills of James Hadley, coloured to simulate stained ivory; 45 cm (18 in), dated 1881.*

CENTRE *The set of six 'Down and Out' characters modelled by Hadley to support menus written on sandwich boards; introduced by Royal Worcester in the 1870s, they enjoyed very widespread popularity. 16 cm (6¼ in) high.*

BELOW *Three from the extensive range of small Royal Worcester figures introduced during the 1880s with hollow bases designed to extinguish candles.*

ABOVE *A group of Royal Worcester porcelain in the Japanesque style, 1875-1880. Some pieces directly copy Japanese orignals, but most combine various oriental themes.* Private collection.

illustrations of Kate Greenaway, are also popular; the prim and proper, slightly mischievous youngsters were brought to life in porcelain by James Hadley's character modelling. Larger groups of two or more children, often supporting candle branches or basket tops, served the same purpose as Dresden ornaments, which enjoyed great popularity in England at the time.

Some English factories, particularly T. & J. Bevington in Staffordshire, made more direct copies of Dresden ornaments, encrusted with flowers and prettily coloured. Others, such as Moore Brothers at Copeland, made figures and lamp bases supported by *putti* and cherubs in white porcelain with details in gilding. Royal Worcester developed its own style of colouring which initially suited the figures of Middle Eastern subjects. A matt enamel realistically simulating ivory was used to good effect on heads and arms of figures, while the costumes, brightly gilded or shaded in bronze or gold, imitated the gilt metalwork on continental bronze and ivory figures. Colourful use of early forms of aerograph sprays produced additional subtle shading. With names like 'prismatic enamels' or 'shot silk', Royal Worcester's figures had become a well established style. It was fortunate that James Hadley was so prolific and versatile as customers called for new models in the latest styles. To be successful, factories had to keep up to date with new techniques; in the 1870s that meant switching dramatically to a whole new artistic influence which was sweeping Europe and enjoying great popularity.

Japan had closed its doors to the West for more than a century; when trade with Europe was re-established in the 1860s, Japanese art created a sensation. Lacquer, metalwork, ivory and ceramics were first displayed in major exhibitions in London in 1862 and Paris in 1867. European manufacturers greatly admired the craftsmanship of the Japanese art. The perfect execution was a model for the leading English factories to try to emulate. Most first attempted some Japanese styles, but three factories whole-heartedly adopted them, striving to prepare major displays to out-do even the Japanese at forthcoming international exhibitions. Minton and Royal Worcester created between them a whole new style which formed a perfect bridge between European and Eastern art. Where the Japanese shapes were not exciting enough, they introduced a few elements from China and India, mixed up with classical ideas. The result was 'Japanesque', Worcester's name for their version of Japanese ceramics which, to English customers, appeared even more Japanese than the oriental originals; it consisted of square vases decorated with fans and scrolls, asymmetrical designs which needed a whole new range of Japanesque furniture on which to display them. The Japanese taste brought with it a completely different style of living, which culminated in the Aesthetic movement of the early 1880s.

At the Vienna Exhibition of 1872 Minton showed turquoise-glazed copies of Japanese shapes and dessert services gilded with cranes in flight, with Mount Fuji in the distance. Worcester exhibited a series of vases, shown here, illustrating the art of porcelain-making in Japan, for which they received almost universal praise. Designed by R. W. Binns, they were modelled cleverly in low relief by James Hadley. The decoration in soft colours, hard bronze, and gold was so carefully copied from Japanese originals that a delegation of Japanese ambassadors, when they visited Worcester in 1872, could not believe that the vases had not been made in Japan.

Generally, examples of Japanesque are very much undervalued. Perhaps because the wares are so strange and alien to British taste today, most of the oriental-style pieces, in spite of their rarity and quality, are much less popular than traditional English styles. Multiple vases formed as linked sections of bamboo, or little posy holders simulating carved ivory or glazed to resemble jade, can be bought cheaply; in many cases, it is hard to find buyers at all. Displayed asymmetrically in groups, in a Japanese setting, such a collection can have a very decorative effect today. Japanesque is an area to watch in the future; I feel sure prices will rise for the best examples of the style produced by Worcester and Minton.

By 1880 the Japanesque style had been completely adapted to suit English taste. Japanesque and Aesthetic styles went hand in hand, the latter being merely an attempt to anglicize the oriental themes. Japanesque emblems became even more stylized, while Aesthetic emblems – a graceful lily and a rigidly symmetrical sunflower – became standard ornaments in fashionable London society. However, the style became something of a joke and the spiritual leader of the Aesthetic movement, Oscar Wilde, was

ABOVE *The Japanese Pottery Story, illustrated on a pair of Royal Worcester vases. 26 cm (10½ in). Modelled by Hadley and painted by James Callowhill in 1872. Japanesque porcelain at its most superb.*

ABOVE *'The Aesthetic Teapot'; a remarkable satire on Oscar Wilde and the Aesthetic Movement. Male on one side, female on the other, the model actually functions as a teapot. 15 cm (6 in), dated 1882.*

parodied by Gilbert and Sullivan in their operetta, *Patience*, which opened in 1881. Society was greatly entertained by this send-up and were happy to buy an expensive cartoon created in porcelain to commemorate the opening production. After R. W. Binns' design, James Hadley modelled the 'Aesthetic Teapot' as a satire on Oscar Wilde and the whole Aesthetic movement. One side depicts a lovesick maiden, the other a soulfully intense young man, and no piece of porcelain sums up the Victorian period better. It is my favourite piece of nineteenth-century porcelain and I have always wanted one. During my fourteen years at Phillips, we have sold five examples and I have watched them rise in price steadily from £300 to £600, then to £1,000. The example illustrated here sold in 1988 for £1,650, evidence of the continuing strength of Victorian quality porcelain.

One area of Japanesque/Aesthetic porcelain which has increased in value and interest in recent years is Minton's copies of *cloisonné*, the enamelled metal vases imported from China and Japan. The factory had for a long time specialized in a rich turquoise enamel ground, and this was gilded and coloured with bold, bright patterns. Some of these designs were created by Dr Christopher Dresser, a

LEFT *The rich turquoise glaze of Minton's*
cloisonné *wares is even more vivid than the*
Japanese originals which were being copied;
the glazed porcelain bases simulate lacquer;
30.5 cm (12 in), c.1880.

major designer of ceramics, glass and metalware. His dramatic
shapes and patterns were intended to be made in factory conditions
so that ordinary people could afford to have good designs. Minton's
cloisonné was not cheap when it was made in the 1880s; for a hundred
years afterwards it was neglected. Only recently have prices begun to
rise noticeably.

The Japanesque movement came to an end as fast as it had
begun. It had been introduced when there was a shortage of original
oriental porcelain in England, but the situation changed dramatically
owing to mass-production in China and Japan of porcelain and
metalwork made specifically for the west. Blue and white and Canton
enamelled porcelain from China, and colourful Satsuma stoneware
vases from Japan were imported in bulk by stores such as Liberty in
London, who sold them at much cheaper prices than the Worcester
or Minton copies. The English factories concentrated instead on
developing the High-Victorian styles; at the same time, makers were
looking ahead to new trends in Europe, heralding the arrival of Art
Nouveau.

A large number of factories were making porcelain in England
at the end of the nineteenth century, mostly in the potteries centred
around Stoke-on-Trent. Some, like Minton, Wedgwood, Copeland
and Worcester made high quality, expensive porcelain as well as
basic, everyday domestic wares, while other factories just produced
commercial dinner, tea, and toilet sets, aimed at the lower classes for
ordinary use. Many cheap sets were decorated with crude copies of
the established patterns made by the bigger factories; copies were
produced of the Imari patterns of Derby and the ivory grounds of

Worcester, in particular. Some can be very decorative; services from the 1890s by the minor makers offer very good value if they are reasonably complete and therefore usable. A good condition set of about a hundred years old can cost far less than any modern tea or dinner service. There is no need to be frightened of using an antique service as, with sensible care, good quality porcelain can stand up perfectly well to modern use, and can give a great deal of pleasure to its owner. Complete tea services by unimportant makers are usually fairly cheap, especially if one or two cups are broken. Local auctions are a good hunting ground for sets like these.

ABOVE *A Derby flower trough c.1880, and two pieces of Minton from the 1870s. The more delicate styles inspired by Europe are in complete contrast to the Japanesque wares popular at the same time.*

Many years after the closure of the Bloor factory, two new porcelain works were established in Derby. They were not direct continuations of the earliest Derby factory, although both were inspired greatly by traditional Derby wares. A porcelain factory was founded in King Street, Derby, in 1859 and continued by Mr. Sampson Hancock from 1861 until 1935. This firm produced mainly copies of early Derby porcelain and little that was original. Across the city, in Osmaston Road, the Derby Crown Porcelain Company was formed in 1876, changing its name to the more commercial Royal Crown Derby in 1890. Specializing, to begin with, in copies of old Derby Imari and Japan patterns, Royal Crown Derby soon established its own style of decoration which remains as popular as ever in the 1980s. Its best-selling patterns, 'Old Witches' and 'The Cigar' pattern, a design named after a similar decoration on the decorative bands around certain cigars, have proved second only to the 'Willow' pattern in their long-standing popularity.

With income from these services, Royal Crown Derby could afford to venture into the unpredictable rich ornamental market. Their passport to the top league involved yet another French artist who had been persuaded to join them from Minton. Desiré Leroy had

painted in the Limoges enamel style at Minton in the 1880s, but had been trained as an all-round decorator. At Derby, he showed that not only could he paint delicate panels of flowers and trophies, but at the same time he applied the ground colours, added the gilding and any raised enamel jewelling himself. A piece signed Leroy is likely to be entirely his own work. The quality is always exceptional, and perhaps for this reason prices have more than doubled in the last three years, the vase illustrated on page 130 selling in September 1988 for £3,500.

From the 1890s onwards, almost all of the painters at Derby, as opposed to just one or two leading artists, were allowed to sign their work. Gradually Coalport and Worcester followed suit, permitting signed work only after about 1900. Earlier pieces are rarely signed and this, of course, is frustrating for the collector.

Coalport developed a very rich, deep blue ground which they used on a wide range of vases as background, in conjunction with creamy yellow borders and gilding. The reserved panels of landscapes by Edward Ball, Percy Simpson or Fred Perry were painted in a more delicate style than some of their counterparts. One speciality at which Coalport excelled was in the making of jewelled porcelain. To apply simulated pearls or turquoises in raised enamel involved a

ABOVE *Four Derby vases from the 1880s and 1890s illustrating just a few of the styles being produced at the time. The quality, particularly of the gilding, is superb throughout.*

great deal of skill. A paste was mixed and applied in a small blob, with a raised point so that during the firing it settled into a perfect turquoise jewel without a sunken centre; too much or too little paste on one drop would spoil the entire, perfectly graduated effect. Values of Coalport jewelled porcelain have risen and fallen unpredictably in the last fifteen years. In 1987 Phillips sold a jewelled ewer for £440, while the same piece would have fetched £600 two years earlier. Today, however, prices have risen again. Fluctuations like this make the job of valuing antique ceramics so terribly difficult. They do show that in any market there are areas which can be undervalued and set to rise rapidly, while others can be over-expensive, with a predictable fall in value to come. Late-nineteenth century wares are much more susceptible to ups and downs in the market than eighteenth century porcelain, which has risen in value more consistently over the years.

The year 1887 marked a most significant event in British history – the golden jubilee of Queen Victoria. Everyone in the country, it seems, wanted a souvenir, and it could not be predicted that ten years later the Diamond Jubilee would prompt a similar demand. While commemorative souvenirs of Victoria's coronation or wedding are reasonably scarce, between them the two jubilees saw an incredible number of mugs, beakers, and plates mass-produced in the potteries at Stoke-on-Trent. Made cheaply, these souvenirs were mostly printed in one colour or hand-coloured over a printed outline. Lithographic printing was a new technique which was set to revolutionize the ceramics industry. Tiny dots of different colours

ABOVE *A Staffordshire plate commemorating the death of Queen Victoria decorated with a photo-litho colour print. This better than average example sold in 1988 for £83.*

RIGHT *A Royal Crown Derby vase decorated by Desiré Leroy, the shape inspired by Art Nouveau although the decoration reverts back, once again, to the glories of early Sèvres. 17 cm (6¾ in), dated 1902.*

were superimposed on each other and applied to the piece of porcelain in a simple transfer. The result resembles a fine hand painting in colouring, except that, when magnified, the design is seen to be made up of the tiny coloured dots, in a manner similar to the reproduction of a photograph in a magazine. The process was ideal for royal commemoratives and, of course, was adopted for general use as the twentieth century developed.

Every factory made Jubilee souvenirs in 1887 and 1897. Most examples from the minor makers in the potteries can form an interesting and affordable collection. The leading factories joined in the widespread trend for producing fine, expensive porcelain alongside cheap ranges to compete with the rest of Staffordshire. Worcester made tens of thousands of plates, while Doulton churned out a seemingly endless number of beakers and mugs. At the top end of the market, Victoria's portrait was added to already popular products such as the Imari patterns at Derby and ivory ground wares at Worcester. There is unlimited scope for collecting later royal souvenirs. In 1988, Phillips sold the extensive collection of royal commemoratives formed by Sir Lincoln Hallinan. All bought relatively recently, the majority of pieces in the collection were not expensive, with most of the Victorian Jubilee commemoratives selling for between £20 and £40 each. The attractive colour-printed plate shown opposite sold for £83. At the other extreme, special pieces such as Coalport's Jubilee Vase – one of a limited edition of one hundred, depicting scenes from the British Empire and highlights of the reign – would fetch a much higher price.

Feelings of imperialism were strong in Victorian England. The influence of the Empire brought a great deal of art and culture from distant countries to public attention. In particular, ivory from India competed with Japanese ivory carving. The stained ivory look was clearly much in demand and many factories made imitations in porcelain. Royal Worcester led the field with its various shaded effects, called 'Old Ivory' and 'Blush Ivory'. Used on most of James Hadley's figures, the factory found the matt-ivory grounds were also very popular on vases and tewares, as a background to flower sprays and birds in coloured-over etchings, picked out in gold. Worcester's stand at the Chicago World's Columbian Exposition in 1893 was dominated by pieces with ivory grounds; these were to remain popular at least until the 1920s. The most successful wares were designed by Edward Raby, who produced a series of etchings which were applied to the ivory ground and then coloured over. Many bear his initials, E.R., hidden in the design, a feature well worth searching for. The ivory-ground style became so popular that it is without a doubt the most copied of all Royal Worcester's products, with imitations mostly made in Germany, Austria and Czechoslovakia. In England it was copied in earthenware by several Staffordshire factories such as Fielding and Company, who used the name 'Crown Devon'. Porcelain copies were made by Doulton, where Edward Raby worked after leaving Worcester in 1894. Even Wedgwood imitated the ivory grounds, but Worcester maintained its position, producing work superior to that of its rivals.

BELOW *A Royal Worcester vase decorated with a hand-coloured engraving after Edward Raby, on a 'blush ivory' ground. 45 cm (18 in), dated 1899. The factory had an enormous output of similar wares, although rarely as large and impressive as this.*

ABOVE *Undoubtedly the finest example of craftsmanship illustrated in this book, the teapot was carved entirely by hand by George Owen. 12.5 cm (5 in) high. Made by Royal Worcester in 1887, it sold in 1980 for £1,020.*

One of their particular specialities was 'pierced ivory'. Both Royal Worcester and Grainger & Co. in Worcester developed a method of piercing delicate vases with intricate patterns inspired by Eastern ivories. The clay was carved whilst still wet, and its tendency to split and distort in the kiln meant that the process could prove expensive. When successful, the effect can be very beautiful, with the addition of shaded-ivory effect or jewelling in colours and gold.

The finest pierced work of all was that produced by George Owen, a quiet and very secretive craftsman who worked at Royal Worcester from the 1870s. Instead of following a moulded outline, as in the normal way of producing ivories, Owen carved his vases by hand and eye alone, producing a honeycomb of delicate porcelain so fine that it is impossible to believe anyone could have made it. I remember selling a fine vase ten years ago for £1,000 and thinking at the time how reasonable this was, considering the months of work George Owen spent on it. In 1988 three equally fine vases broke through the £10,000 barrier, fetching prices way beyond those for other late-Victorian English porcelain. No other porcelain artist

ABOVE *Fine 'reticulated' porcelain made by the Grainger factory in Worcester, 1885-1895. Carved while the clay is still wet, the piercing follows a moulded outline and should be compared with the work of George Owen, who used no such guidelines (opposite).*

before or since has come close to Owen's achievement, and, while his vases may be too ornate for many people's taste, nobody can fail to marvel at the genius which created them.

It is appropriate to bring the history of English porcelain in the eighteenth and nineteenth centuries to an end on such a high note. Victorian taste had settled down and the flamboyant extravagances of the 1890s contrasted with a new style of art from Europe which was represented in England by new styles of pottery and stoneware. Art Nouveau was, however, mostly ignored by English porcelain makers. Worcester tried out a few designs, but their traditional customers did not buy them and they were soon inspired by Art Nouveau from Vienna, but these were manufactured in glazed pottery rather than porcelain. Artistry in ceramics now became dominated by pottery. Doulton, and many other firms, used porcelain only for traditional wares; art potteries such as Moorcroft, De Morgan, and the Martin Brothers avoided porcelain altogether. The only exceptions were 'Sabrina' ware at Worcester and 'Titanian' ware from Doulton, porcelains which were stained with almost random glaze effects.

Occasionally very beautiful, these glaze effects were really more suited to pottery and the porcelain makers soon reverted to their more traditional lines. The death of Queen Victoria saw the passing of an era; the Edwardian age brought with it a much more complacent air. The excitement which had built the Empire and the strength and genius which had brought about such great technological advances in the early-Victorian period had all but disappeared by the end of the nineteenth century. The sense of urgency had passed, and English manufacturers rested on their laurels. In 1900 R. W. Binns died. He had been the guiding force at Worcester for nearly fifty years and his death was followed three years later by that of James Hadley. Worcester relied on the ivory wares and Hadley figures for the next twenty years and introduced little that was new and original. Derby continued to make the Imari wares and traditional painted pieces, and again proved reluctant to up-date or introduce new ranges. The same was true of Coalport, Copeland/Spode and, insofar as their porcelain was concerned, Minton and Doulton. The only area which can be singled out for praise is the work of certain individual artists – at Worcester and Doulton, in particular – who brought a degree of impressionism into their paintings. Harry Davis and the Stinton family at Worcester, William Dean at Derby, and George Evans at Doulton are all names worthy of mention, but lie beyond the scope of this book, being artists of the twentieth century. More than one hundred and fifty years on from the first crude attempts at English porcelain, we are left with a rich heritage to admire and collect.

Chapter Thirteen
Hints on Collecting English Porcelain

IDENTIFICATION

While it is possible to collect according to shape, style or purely personal taste, it is natural to want to identify the maker of any piece in your collection. This may seem quite straigthforward, and it is certainly true that most people who queue to have their porcelain identified at an 'Antiques Roadshow' expect to be told exactly who made every piece. The problem, of course, is that right up until the middle of the Victorian period only a minority of pieces of English porcelain bare a maker's mark. As you read through the chapters of this book you will get some idea of the original research carried out over the years in factory archives, archaeological excavations, and museum collections, making the identification of a great deal more English porcelain now possible. There is still a long way to go, and while experts still argue over the true attributions of many pieces, you may wonder how on earth a novice can begin to tell different makes apart.

A factory mark is, of course, the greatest clue. In a recent sale of good English porcelain at Phillips, of the pieces made during the period under consideration, only one third bore the genuine mark of the maker. The rest were unmarked or simply designated with a pattern number or workman's tally mark, while 4 per cent included copies of Chinese or Meissen marks. The pieces with a factory mark almost all originated from just three factories: Chelsea, Worcester and Derby, the most successful English makers and also the three most copied. Fakes of products from these factories far out-number any other forgeries, and so it becomes clear that any marks on English porcelain have to be treated with more suspicion than trust (see Chapter 14, on fakes). The marks most often copied are the Chelsea anchor, the crescent of Worcester, and the crowned 'D' of Derby, all simple to paint. Incised, impressed or printed marks are very rarely copied, and this is an important point to remember. When the printed mark of Rockingham was forged in France, for example, the fakes bore a hand-painted copy, not finely engraved like the original. Printed Royal Worcester or Royal Crown Derby marks, for example, or impressed Wedgwood or Minton marks, are extremely unlikely to be anything other than genuine.

If a piece is unmarked or bears only a painted mark, it needs to be considered in the light of other evidence before a firm attribution can be made. The first thing any expert will do is look at the style of the shape or decoration. Porcelain usually reflects the styles in art popular at the time the piece was made – the principal changes in taste and style have been discussed in chronological order throughout this book. A tureen of pure classical Roman or Greek shape is likely to date from the neo-classical period from 1775 to about 1800, and would not be made before 1770; a very flamboyant ornament reviving the style of the Renaissance will almost certainly be High Victorian, from the third quarter of the nineteenth century. Some styles, such as pure Japanesque or aesthetic can be closely dated to around 1875-1885. The rococo style can be more difficult to date as it was popular from 1750-1780, and again during the period 1825-1845.

The next step is to consider the body and glaze. Eighteenth-century rococo porcelain will be of an artificial soft paste variety, while neo-rococo pieces from the 1830s will be manufactured in a form of bone china. Sadly, it is impossible to put into words in this book any real clues to identify the differences between the pastes and glazes of various factories. Some particular characteristics of each factory's wares have been listed in the general section on makers at the back of this book. There are general features to look out for – such as the rough appearance of eighteenth century gilding, made by mixing gold with honey, compared with the much smoother, brighter effect achieved when mercury was mixed with gold on most later-eighteenth and nineteenth-century pieces. Similarly, look out for

the high quality and evenness of finely-mixed ground colours on nineteenth-century dessert services and vases, in contrast to the more uneven, mottled background colours that appear on early Worcester or Derby.

All these differences and characteristics can be learnt only by close examination of actual examples; there is no short cut to picking up the skills which porcelain experts eventually find instinctive. After nearly fifteen years of handling something in the order of one million pieces of ceramics at Phillips, I rarely have to think twice about whether a pieces is soft or hard paste porcelain. The more you handle, the easier it becomes. Shapes and pattern number sequences can be a little easier to learn and, with reference to the right books, it is possible for anyone to identify certain unmarked pieces without too much difficulty. A library of all the books listed in this guide will enable most pieces to be attributed in some way or another, and the detective work needed can be both enjoyable and frustrating at times. Cup handle shapes can identify a maker only if exactly the same shape is illustrated in a book – and even then some shapes were made by more than one firm.

Many nineteenth-century tea and dinner wares are marked only with a number which corresponds with the factory's own pattern lists. Pattern numbers can be used more often to rule out makers who did not make a particular example than to give a positive attribution to a piece. A simple number such as 1562, for example, on a shape made around 1820, shows that the shape could not have been made at Coalport, whose numbers did not go above a thousand. Equally, this number would exclude Flight of Worcester and Derby, who did not use pattern numbers at this time. But the piece could still originate from any of a large number of Staffordshire makers who simply used a progressive pattern number sequence. Some factories used fractional numbers at different times – such as 2/55, which could be Coalport, Grainger, Ridgway, or Rockingham, amongst others; equally 5/960 could well be Ridgway, but not exclusively. Pattern numbers must, therefore, be studied in conjunction with the shape of the piece. Some numbers can be confirmed by contacting the factories, where many pattern books still survive.

Once you have tried, as far you can, to identify a maker, it may be necessary to seek expert help and this, sadly, may be difficult. Most museums offer some form of identification service, although only a few of the larger institutions have specialists who can identify some of the minor makers of English porcelain. Various groups organize forms of valuation days and 'roadshows', where items can be taken for an opinion, but, again, these opinions are only as reliable as the specialists available. The BBC 'Antiques Roadshows' are the largest of the mobile valuation events organized around the country, but opinions can only be given if you are prepared to turn up on the day and stand in a queue. Most fine art auctioneers have porcelain specialists and are willing to give opinions, although they tend to be professional valuers who can only offer a free identification service to those who are willing to sell with them. At branches of Phillips the specialists are quite happy to advise customers about items offered in their sales and can give guidance on forming collections. We are pleased to identify occasional pieces of porcelain for you, although there would be a charge for a full inventory or valuation of a collection unless it was requested with a view to sell.

The best way to be confident about the identification of items in your collection is to learn as much as you can about the subject and to buy from reliable sources whenever possible.

COLLECTING

Anyone wishing to collect porcelain would be limited only by the funds available and the room for display. There are many ways to collect, entirely dependent on personal taste. In a purely general way, you can buy any items which you think attractive and affordable, regardless of maker or period. In this way you could form a very personal collection which is enjoyable to live with – although this sort of collecting can get a little out of control and not everything can live happily together!

In the specific field of English porcelain the most usual approach is to collect the work of one factory. It is possible to choose a rare or short-lived factory and seek any example you can find, regardless of quality or condition. If you collect the wares of a large factory like Worcester or Derby, you will be faced with enormous choice and must limit your collection in some way to a period or type of decoration. Some factories, like Chelsea or Swansea and Nantgarw, will always be expensive and hard to find, while the products of other

factories can range from remarkably inexpensive items to rare and costly ones. An interest in one factory can become fairly obsessive; it is possible to became a considerable authority on the history of one factory by studying the wares and carrying out original research yourself – finding an unknown piece of information can be extremely satisfying, and many major discoveries have been made by keen and dedicated amateurs.

The two other ways of collecting are by style or shape. Concentrating on a particular form of decoration, such as blue and white, is a very popular way to collect. Examples from all of the different factories can be gathered and the colour of the blue and quality of painting or printing contrasted. Other styles to be considered are chinoiserie and oriental influences; Imari and Japan patterns can form the basis of a very stunning collection; flower-encrusted and pretty neo-rococo styles, parian figures and groups constitute another area; alternatively, Japanesque wares of the 1880s are a much neglected field. The list of subjects is endless, offering very great scope. The important thing is to choose something you like and are happy to live with.

The final major collecting area is by subject; in collecting one type of ware you have only to buy examples which attract you. Teapots are an obvious subject, and there are very many dedicated teapot enthusiasts about. Almost as popular are cups and saucers; or else you can collect jugs, or plates, or any other single shape. Useful objects of the past are fun to hunt out and collect. In 1989 Phillips sold the collection of the late Sylvia Watkins, who had specialized in small candlesticks, inkwells and baskets in English porcelain. Cataloguing the many hundreds of delightful objects for the sale was as interesting to me as it must have been to Mrs Watkins as she bought each new example over a lifetime of collecting. The illustration on page 135 shows just a small selection of her pieces which sold at auction for considerably more than they would have cost when she originally bought them. Again, this sort of collecting can get out of hand, and it is necessary to watch for quality. Buying anything, for example teapots, simply in order to amass the largest number of items ever gathered together, is pure obsession. It is much better to have 25 nice teapots instead of a 125 ordinary ones – and, in the long term, the better examples will give more pleasure and prove a much better investment.

WHERE TO BUY

Once you have decided what it is you want to collect, the main problem is finding examples at the right price. It is all very well to dream about coming across just what you are looking for at a bargain price at a jumble or car-boot sale, but, sadly, this rarely happens. There is nothing to lose by looking through the boxes of bric-à-brac in a junk shop; every collector will show you favourite pieces found in just this way. A collection with a theme, however, needs to be hunted down more carefully, and cannot be built up in a hurry. Patience is a very important quality in a good collector.

There are three main places to buy English porcelain – antique shops, antique fairs and auction rooms. In all cases you have the chance to pit your skills and knowledge against the person selling and, if you know your subject well enough, you can make a good buy even in the most expensive gallery or highly publicized sale. Most collectors do need some sort of guidance and there is no shortage of people willing to give advice. The quality of advice can vary, however, and buyers do have to proceed with great care.

Antique fairs are, in effect, many small or specialized antique shops rolled into one. As the cost of running a shop becomes so high, dealers can attract more customers by gathering together at a large venue either for a one day fair, usually held on a Sunday, or else for a more specialized event spread over two or more days. Some local fairs are little more than junk markets where a high proportion of the goods on offer are either of poor quality or are modern reproductions. Sadly, this type of event has affected the reputation of the higher class fair, where it is possible to buy very high quality items from specialist dealers. There has been a recent trend for fairs purely devoted to ceramics, where all of the exhibitors sell just pottery, porcelain and glass. At the top venues, these fairs bring together the very best porcelain dealers from all over the country; wealthy collectors and foreign dealers jostle with local trade and 'just-interested' small time collectors to get to the front of the queue and have first chance to buy some of the finest English ceramics.

If you are still a newcomer, it is safest to go to a fair which has been 'vetted' by a panel of experts, to weed out any obvious forgeries or heavily restored items. At all times, however, you will be at the mercy of the dealer who is selling the porcelain.

While some dealers are very knowledgeable and totally reliable, a great many who sell at antiques fairs or through their own shops can be little more than general traders themselves, with only an amateur knowledge of English porcelain. I am frequently astounded by some of the attributions given to items in fairly respectable shops or fairs, usually sold in perfectly good faith by dealers who know no better.

The general rule of buying from a reputable dealer is sound advice, but is meaningless when there is no way of telling just how knowledgeable a dealer really is. However honest and trustworthy a dealer may be, the best protection against making a serious mistake is to ask for a receipt which states what the item you are buying is, roughly when it was made, and any damage or restoration which may not be visible. Any reputable dealer will be perfectly willing to give this, and many do so as a matter of course. Keep your receipts safely, and if at any time in the future you find the item is not as it had been described, then you will be able to take it back and be in a strong position to demand a refund.

From my experience, I have found only a very few dealers to be deliberately dishonest; most dealers want to retain the custom of collectors and try to be as open as possible. Friendships will develop easily between keen collectors and specialist dealers with the same interests, and such relationships can be very beneficial to both parties, the collector willing to pay a little bit extra for the dealer's knowledge and ability to locate special pieces in small auctions all over the country.

Apart from the uncertainty over the price you will have to pay, buying at auction is similar to buying from a dealer. There is a world of difference between a local bric-à-brac sale run by a charity, or perhaps controlled by small general dealers, and a major fine art auction in the centre of London. At the lowest end of the market, when a sale has no formal catalogue or conditions, there is little chance of protecting yourself against being misled. Any established auction firm which produces a printed catalogue is responsible for the way goods are described and, although it can sometimes be difficult to enforce, the law is there to protect the buyer. The same general advice about buying from dealers and fairs applies to buying at auction. There is much less chance of making a killing and spotting something no one else has seen at a quality London auction than at a small local sale, but the extra price you may have to pay at a good auction is balanced by the guarantees which apply to every reputable auctioneer.

At a London auction, such as Phillips, there is a premium of 10 per cent of the hammer price to be paid by the purchaser; this is common practice now in the majority of British salesrooms. In return, the buyer gets the chance to come to a single sale and find several hundred good lots of pottery and porcelain fully and accurately described by some of the country's leading experts. Many people still feel auction rooms are the domain of dealers, but nowadays more and more private collectors come to the salerooms themselves and compete with the dealers who used to supply them. Buying at auction is not necessarily cheaper than buying in a shop or fair, and can even work out dearer. Often though, a dealer has to allow a sufficient margin for profit in his final bid, and a private buyer can save paying the dealer his commission.

At auction there is some opportunity to view an item before the sale, and usually a lot more time to decide on your price than in the hustle and bustle of an antique fair. At any leading auction firm there is always a specialist on hand somewhere behind the scenes, usually the expert who catalogued the lot in which you may be interested.

We are always perfectly happy to advise any potential buyer on the merits of any lot and, much more importantly, can discuss any damage which may not be visible. All London auctioneers now mention damage in their catalogues, or at least indicate where damage has been disguised by restoration. We have nothing to hide and are glad to point out to a buyer any defect, as well as discuss why we have given an item its estimated price.

Smaller auctioneers and many provincial branches do not mention damage, and if you discover that you have acquired a piece without realizing it was cracked or damaged, there is little you can do. A dealer will tell you of any known damage to an item before selling it; small auction houses do not have to, but if you ask a cataloguer or saleroom porter, they will usually be perfectly willing to tell you of any defects they know about on any given lot. Where damage or restoration is mentioned in the catalogue, as a general rule the buyer has a reasonable right to a refund if the lot turns out to be repaired or damaged and this was not indicated.

The most important thing to remember when buying, from whatever source, is to trust your own judgement as much as anything, and buy only something that gives you pleasure or fills a gap in your collection. This way, with a little care and common sense, you will not go far wrong.

VALUES

This is the most difficult area to write about or to understand. So many factors can affect the value of an item that nobody can confidently predict what any one person is prepared to pay for it. The biggest subject of conversation every Monday morning among antiques dealers and collectors is the value placed on objects by experts on the 'Antiques Roadshow' shown on BBC television the day before. On the programme, experts from auction rooms or the antiques trade give a personal opinion of the value of an item. I remember my father, Henry Sandon, discussing on one particular programme the value of a miniature chamber pot made at the Caughley factory in about 1780. It had been bought for 50 pence at a car boot sale; the lucky owner who had bought it was told it was worth more than £1,000. The following week almost every dealer in London who came to my sale of porcelain at Phillips told me what a ridiculously high value this was. The miniature potty turned up for sale at Christie's in London a few months later and doubled its pre-sale estimate to sell for £1,370. This was the price two keen collectors were prepared to pay for it, and who are we in the auction business to argue with that?

The point of this story is that if you ask ten English porcelain collectors, or dealers for that matter, to give a value on a particular item, the chances are you will get ten different prices. Something that is common, an example of which turns up for sale every few weeks, can be valued with little difficulty on the strength of other examples sold recently. When no similar item has been sold for several years, how can anyone know for certain what it is likely to fetch? We all read newspaper reports of an important Impressionist painting selling for three or five times its pre-sale estimate. The same happens, to a lesser extent, with sales of English porcelain, and, while I am always delighted when a piece sells for an exceptional price, it is nice sometimes to find that pieces just make their estimate and I am proved right in my valuation.

Market trends – popularity of a particular

item or style at a given moment – are most important in determining value, and this can never be predicted scientifically. The value of any item is affected by many things, but three factors in particular should be considered when deciding the value of a piece of porcelain. These factors are rarity, quality, and, in its own way, beauty. None of these on its own will automatically make a piece valuable; value is often dependent on a combination of all three.

Some early porcelains, experimental or crudely made, appear to have very little quality and, to most people, are not particularly beautiful either. Yet, because of their rarity, they are valuable, and therefore have a new kind of beauty in the eyes of collectors. Other pieces can be terribly rare or even unique but, unless they appeal to collectors who want to own them, their rarity will not be reflected in the amount anyone is prepared to pay. When buying porcelain do not be misled about its value because a piece is rare. Unless it is well made and interesting enough to you, and you want to live with it, a piece is not always worth buying for its rarity alone. Many items are rare simply because no one was prepared to buy them when they were made, and they appear similarly unattractive today. The most popular patterns or figures are inevitably more common today and often the prices these realize do not reflect the craftsmanship and quality which went into them. An experienced collector understands rarity. A beginner is best advised to let his own taste govern his choice and only to buy a piece because he likes it.

Learning values in order to know what you should pay is the most difficult part of collecting and there is no substitute for experience. Price guides, such as Miller's or Lyle's, undoubtedly help, but can also mislead. The only answer is to visit as many shops, antique fairs, and auctions as possible, view the porcelain and compare prices. Only then will you be able to estimate whether you are paying a fair price or a price over the odds. You can then learn to spot the bargains which lie in every sale or fair.

CONDITION

By its very nature, porcelain is fragile and prone to damage; indeed, this is why certain pieces are special and rare today. There is no doubt that any damage must devalue a piece of porcelain, although in many instances it is more a case of a premium payable for the few examples which have survived intact. Every collector views damage in a different way and it is, therefore, impossible to generalize on how damage affects value. Chips are perfectly acceptable on an English delft dish, for example, because of the ultra soft body; the slightest crack in a piece of Chinese porcelain, on the other hand, removes most of its value.

My advice to any collector is to avoid damage if you can. This means that if a piece is relatively common, and by waiting a few months a perfect example could be found, it is not worth buying the damaged one, unless, perhaps, it is 10 pence in your local jumble sale! On the other hand, if a piece is rare and you are unlikely to come across another, why dismiss it simply on the grounds that it is slightly damaged?

I know of many collectors who will never buy a damaged piece. While I can understand this attitude, I do not regard such a person as a true collector. Most of my favourite pieces in my own collection are damaged, but they are superb examples of the workmanship of leading factories or artists. The only way many smaller collectors can afford to buy the finest early Chelsea or Worcester is if the pieces are badly damaged. Of course it is not the same as when a piece is perfect, but Jefferyes Hammett O'Neale's painting is just as fine on a broken Chelsea teapot as on a perfect one for ten times the price. Quality pieces, if bought for a broken price, will hold their value just as well as perfect ones. Ordinary wares, damaged, will never prove a worthwhile investment.

For this reason it is far better to buy just a few good pieces each year – either perfect or damaged quality items – rather than a much larger number of less expensive pieces. This means that your collection will grow rather more slowly, but in the long run it will give you much more pleasure and probably prove a much better investment. As a youngster and beginner myself, I remember Geoffrey Godden, an important collector and authority on English porcelain, advising me to do just this; his own reference collection was formed in this way. He bought the best English porcelain, regardless of damage, if the quality and rarity was there. In recent years, as his collection has been slowly dispersed, his advice has proved very well founded, with badly damaged but important pieces selling alongside the best of any factory for a great deal more than when he bought them. The important thing to remember is to buy a damaged piece only when you are aware of the full extent of the damage and only to pay a price which reflects this damage.

RESTORATION

Porcelain restoration has become a booming industry in recent years. There are many ways to look at the subject and few people will ever agree on it. I see both the advantages and the disadvantages and certainly a lot of care has to be taken before a decision is made to have a damaged piece repaired.

Basically, there are two sorts of restoration. One is conservation, wherein cracks are sealed to prevent them worsening and missing pieces are made up so that the defect is not disfiguring. Disfigurement is the most important word with respect to restoration. I once bought a Worcester teapot which I knew to be very rare – indeed it still is the only recorded example of the pattern. It was cheap because the end of the spout was missing. Every time I looked at that pot it bothered me, for the proportions and balance of the shape were totally spoilt. I took it to a good restorer and had the bad spout replaced in plaster and paint. Sure, I knew it was restored, but the imbalance was corrected and my eye was drawn to the beauty of the decoration rather than the truncated spout. This is a very beneficial restoration which is perfectly acceptable to any collector.

The other sort of restoration is purely cosmetic – to make a piece seem perfect again when it is not. A bad crack is disfiguring, and to fill and blend it in is one thing; to spray the piece all over with silicon varnish as if there never had been any damage is, to my mind, an extreme measure. A decorative piece of nineteenth-century porcelain with unsightly damage should be restored if it is economical. An eighteenth-century piece is different: while an early Worcester cup looks smarter with the cracks filled in, the spray completely hides the natural feel of the glaze and enamelling. When Phillips sell at auction a piece that is very restored, the buyer usually strips off the repainting almost immediately. The vendor may have spent a considerable sum on the repair and this money will have been wasted. Some pieces will sell for less money after restoration than with the honest damage showing.

Good restoration is as skillful as any ceramic craftsmanship and I am frequently amazed at the unbelievable quality of the best repairs. All of the best experts in the country are deceived now and again by professional restoration. If this is the case, how on earth can a beginner be expected to recognize when a piece has been expertly restored?

The answer is to buy only from reputable sources and, in every case, ask for a receipt stating whether there has been any repair. Auctioneers do not have to disclose restoration, although the law does offer some protection. Do ask a member of the auction staff, preferably the cataloguer, if there has been any repair. It could save you from a costly mistake.

CARE AND DISPLAY

The old cliché still holds good: 'If in doubt, don't'. A great many pieces of porcelain are scruffy when you buy them and it is natural to want to clean them up. Surface dirt should be removed with a damp cloth and only mild detergent. This alone can make a major difference. Anything further requires great care.

If a piece has only underglaze decoration, or is purely white, then no harm can come to it if you use a cream cleaner or detergent to remove all of the surface dirt. Any overglaze decoration can be seriously effected by such cleaning, and you have to take the risk that damage to the decoration could look worse than the original dirt and grime. If you soak a piece, never use anything stronger than a biological washing powder. Many dealers advocate the use of bleach, or more significantly, hydrogen peroxide, to remove staining and dirt from cracks. Bleach, unquestionably, has an effect on glaze and can make the staining worse. Peroxide can clean many pieces but does, in some cases, loosen the glaze and cause enamels or gold to flake off. If you are buying a slightly discoloured piece, steer well clear if you can smell bleach, and never be afraid to ask a dealer if a piece has, to his knowledge, been chemically cleaned. Avoid it if there is any doubt, as the side-effects of such cleaning, particularly bleach, can take several months to emerge, as the gold turns purple and the glaze flakes off.

When displaying porcelain at home the choice is purely personal. I favour grouping pieces closely together in a cabinet, while others prefer a more spacious, museum-like display. Figures, for example, can be grouped in small conversations, just as they would have ornamented an eighteenth-century dessert table. Plates take up a lot of space and can be hung on walls as long as a plastic coated plate-hanger exactly suited to the size of the plate is used. A plate-stand on a wall-bracket is much safer than any wire hanger, which can cause stress and cracking in early ceramics. Old, tightly fitting hanging wires should be removed carefully with a hacksaw, rather than being prised off. It is important that your collection is displayed at an even temperature, away from strong sources of heat or severe cold. A vase on a cold window-sill suddenly subjected to the heat of the sun can crack open for no apparent reason, as stresses build up. I remember hearing from a collector who bought an expensive porcelain dessert service which had been stored in the cold cellar of a country house and sold at an auction in a marquee in the grounds. He took it home and placed it proudly in an illuminated display case. Under the heat of the lamps, within a couple of days six of the plates had split open, with a resounding 'ping' every so often: an extreme case, but one which should serve as a warning. If you are moving porcelain on a cold day, wrap it up very thickly in plenty of newspaper.

Above all, a collection should be personal and if you prefer to have your pieces on open shelves or table tops around a room, then this is fine. It is important to remember the period in which your pieces were made and that some styles work better on country-style oak furniture than on polished Georgian pieces. Japanesque or chinoiserie styles belong on eastern lacquer, while High-Victorian designs need equally outrageous furniture. An average example, displayed sympathetically, can be much more effective than a really fine piece poorly exhibited.

LEARNING ABOUT PORCELAIN

There is no substitute for experience, and the only real way to learn about different factories, bodies and glazes is to handle actual examples. Visiting antique fairs, shops and particularly auctions, enables any collector to handle fine porcelain and thus learn to distinguish fine quality from mediocre. Museums are important for viewing fine examples, but it is not quite the same without the opportunity to handle a piece. The best museums, such as the Victoria and Albert in London, and specialist museums such as those at the porcelain factories at Worcester, Derby, Spode, Minton, and Wedgwood, have wonderful collections arranged chronologically and offer great opportunity to study the wares of a factory systematically.

It is impossible to obtain all of the books necessary to research English porcelain thoroughly. At the end of this section I list general and specialist books which I recommend, although many are now out of print. Good art libraries can get hold of most of these books, while others can be bought from specialist book dealers. Specialist auction catalogues are an inexpensive way to learn, particularly as a guide to values, and there are numerous antiques magazines which regularly carry articles about porcelain. Finally, there are many antique collectors' societies and specialist ceramic circles and societies open to members interested in furthering research into English porcelain. Specialist dealers and museums can often provide details of such groups.

Chapter Fourteen
Fakes and Forgeries

BELOW *A pair of European figurines bearing gold anchor marks reproducing the style of Chelsea. Normally called 'Samson', these lack the quality to attribute them definitely to the great French factory and they were probably made in Germany.*

While so much of the earliest English porcelain directly copied Chinese, German and French wares, and all of the eighteenth-century factories reproduced their rivals' wares, it is not surprising that identifying different factories is far from easy. My concern in this section is with deliberate attempts to deceive with fakes made at a later date. The popularity and value of English porcelain meant that it was worthwhile to make copies as long ago as the 1830s and 1840s. By this time the rococo styles had came back into vogue at Coalport and Worcester. Copies of early Chelsea and Worcester were made as legitimate revivals. Today, one hundred and fifty years old themselves, these are some of the most confusing copies facing collectors. The body and glaze will be different, and colours and gilding are often brighter, but it is not surprising

that these wares frequently deceive.

During the 1840s Lady Charlotte Schreiber, one of the first serious collectors of English porcelain, visited a porcelain manufactory at St Armand-les-Eaux in France, where the soft paste formula previously used at Tournai in the eighteenth century was revived for copies of Sèvres, Chelsea and Worcester. Being soft paste, these copies have a very English feel to them and the quality is outstanding. In particular, Chelsea mazarine blue grounds with tooled gold figures, birds and insects and Worcester ovoid vases with fabulous bird panels on blue scale grounds were reproduced. These vases were reasonably common, and yet they frequently fool fairly knowledgeable people. Six such vases were shown to me during 1988, all firmly believed to be genuine: Two had been bought for considerable sums and I was unable to convince the owners that they had in fact been deceived.

The most prolific maker of fakes was a firm in Paris which specialized in copies of every sort of porcelain, enamel and faience. Edme Samson et Cie made high quality reproductions, particularly of Chinese, German and French porcelain, and the vast range and quantity of their products never ceases to amaze me. They copied all of the popular eighteenth-century early English porcelains, such as Chelsea figures and wares, Bow and Derby figure groups, Worcester blue scale grounds, and Plymouth and Bristol teawares. Every so often one comes across a new sort of Samson fake not seen before – such as copies of Worcester and Lowestoft blue and white, Derby fruit and flower painting or Japan and Imari patterns from Derby or Worcester.

Samson naturally copied the marks of the original factories, but they did also use their own mark of the letter 'S' crossed, occasionally to be found hidden away inside the foot-rim or amongst the scrollwork on the base of a figure. Marked pieces are the exception rather than the rule, but they do help to verse the collector in the high quality of Samson's reproductions. I reluctantly have to admit to having been totally fooled by good Samson copies on several occasions, although in these cases, they were pretending to be German, and the whiteness of the hard paste formula used by Samson closely resembled Meissen and other factories. The French copies of English porcelain are in hard paste rather than the original soft paste used by all English firms except Plymouth and Bristol. Yet, as I explained in earlier chapters, it takes time and experience to learn to tell the two pastes apart. When Samson went so far as to copy irregularities of the originals, especially the blurred effects of blue and white, it is easy to see why so many collectors are still being deceived. The fakes can be more than one hundred years old themselves, and will have developed a certain amount of natural wear and surface dirt in that time.

Many other German and French factories copied English porcelain, especially another Paris maker called Boquillion, who specialized in Chinese armorial decoration and Chelsea and Worcester wares. Many of the minor German copies are particularly cheap and nasty, and there is a tendency to call any continental copy of English porcelain 'Samson' – in most cases such an attribution is made without good reason.

The most common sort of fakes, which are remarkably plentiful, are figures marked with the red or gold anchor of Chelsea. By the 1920s and 1930s the stage had been reached whereby a gold anchor was placed on the back of almost every commercially produced Dresden or French figurine, whether they were copying original Chelsea models or not. The trend continues, with many cheap china ornaments made in the Far East today still bearing a prominent gold anchor on the base. I am sure that less than one in a thousand figures bearing a Chelsea mark have any chance of being genuine.

There are many other sorts of fake porcelain in existence, with new types of very skillful reproductions appearing every year. I have recently been fooled by several very clever fakes sold at auction for considerable sums – until too many started to turn up and the penny dropped! Fakes will always be with us, and all collectors need to be on their guard.

Two types of fake English porcelain, however, are much harder to detect than any others: the so-called 'Torquay' reproductions and genuine porcelain which has been altered or redecorated at a later date.

The true story of the pottery at Torquay has never been unravelled. Many older dealers claim to have known of a man who worked in Torquay in the 1930s or 1950s making clever copies of early English figures, and there are plenty of examples around to prove that someone, somewhere, was quite successful. The body used was an underfired white clay, more pottery than porcelain. However, when copying thick, early English figures, the lack of translucency is not really noticeable. The most common 'Torquay' fakes are pairs of deer or boars after early Derby originals, and in over fifteen years I have seen several dozen of these. Not as finely modelled as the originals, they should not fool anyone familiar with the real thing, but they can be very confusing when they turn up in provincial auction rooms, dirty and often damaged. I have known a pair of boars to sell for £1,000. Much more convincing are small birds on stumps or pairs of Mansion House Dwarfs and one particular pair of harlequin candlesticks which provoked great controversy a few years ago, with some experts refusing to accept that they could be fake while others were convinced of it. The 'Indiscreet

*A Samson cup and saucer unusually copying
Worcester of the 1790s. The hard paste body
gives it away as it is much whiter than the
original.*

Harlequin' shown on page 146, a straightforward
copy of a Bow group, fooled me ten years ago when
it was left for sale at Phillips. My colleagues smelt a
rat and investigated further. The colouring was
very bright, but then Bow often is. I feel sure that a
lot of small collectors or local dealers would be very
excited if such a group turned up in a provincial
saleroom. Fortunately the very best Torquay fakes
are almost as rare as the originals, and would be
well worth collecting in their own right, as long as
you pay the price for a fake.

Copies from Samson or Torquay can be
detected because the body and glaze will be wrong.
It is much more difficult to tell when the porcelain
is original eighteenth century while the decoration
has been added later. In the 1770s there was a

shortage of white porcelain for china painters to
enamel. Some artists, probably in London, bought
Worcester and Caughley porcelain with simple
decoration, slight flower sprays or a little bit of
gilding, and removed the original patterns with acid
or by grinding. In its place, much more elaborate
decoration was added, and it is likely that the
enamelling firm of James Giles, in London, carried
out some redecoration. A century or so later, richly
coloured Worcester had already become highly
collectable, and some of the richest and most
valuable patterns were copied onto Worcester
porcelain devoid of its original design. So there are
two problems confronting the collector: first, has
the piece been redecorated, and if so, was this
over-painting done at the time or was it in fact

applied in the late-nineteenth century?

With high values at stake, this is understandably a controversial area. Some pieces have been, quite obviously, redecorated, and many are rightly condemned as fake. Falling into the grey area are pieces which have little or no signs of any re-firing, but which match up with other pieces which have burnt during a subsequent firing. When a piece of porcelain has been in use for a while, dirt and moisture will be absorbed through the unglazed foot-rim. If it is subsequently fired to fuse the enamelling, this dirt will burst through the surface in a mass of black dots and bubbles. Some pieces will exhibit this blackening after only a few months exposure and a piece may be perfectly genuine and yet still have a blackened foot-rim. Other items can be re-fired after a hundred years and still appear perfectly glazed. The presence of blacking on a foot-rim is usually an indication that a piece has been redecorated, but in no way is such evidence conclusive that the decoration is of a later date.

The biggest clue to look out for, apart from blackening, is when a piece is overcrowded, and the removal of part of the enamelling will result in a popular, more simple pattern. Such doubts have thrown many spanners into the market for richly coloured Worcester, and many expensive items sold maybe twenty years ago as genuine are now believed to be fakes.

With leading experts disagreeing in many cases, how can any novice hope to buy coloured Worcester with confidence? Sadly, there is no easy answer, but a need for natural trust between the collector and dealer and a willingness to keep an open mind. It is better to turn down an important piece if you are in any way unhappy, rather than be saddled with a very expensive mistake if you find no one else will accept it.

I feel reluctant to leave this guide on such a cautionary note. In practice, fakes in English porcelain are nothing like so widespread as in other areas of fine art and antiques, and most are pretty blatant. As you gain experience, most will become quite obvious, and the tricky ones will also start to stand out and give you reason to seek other opinions. Do heed the warnings, however, and never accept anything at face value. Examples of Royal Worcester or Derby printed marks are probably being added to wares at this very moment, some from the correct factory, others purely in their style. New fakes will turn up, but buy wisely and

safely, keeping your receipts, and they should not be a problem. Certainly never let such fears spoil your enjoyment of collecting porcelain.

ABOVE *'The Indiscreet Harlequin' from the class of fakes attributed to Torquay. A sophisticated model in its own right, and a type known to deceive a great many specialists.*

Appendix 1

A List of the Most Important English Porcelain Factories in the Eighteenth and Nineteenth Centuries

In preparing this list it has been necessary to be very selective. Most of the makers are covered in greater detail in the text, but the purpose here is to record for each factory approximate dates, important marks and standard reference works. Some of the books are now out of print, but most good libraries should be able to obtain copies.

To begin with, I propose to list a number of general books which I use constantly at Phillips:

General Bibliography
Berthoud, Michael, *An Anthology of British Cups*, Micawber, 1982.
Bradshaw, Peter, *Eighteenth Century English Porcelain Figures*, Antique Collectors Club, 1981
Cushion, John and Honey, William, *Handbook of Pottery and Porcelain Marks*, Faber, 1980.
Godden, Geoffrey, *Eighteenth Century English Porcelain*, Granada, 1985; *Encyclopaedia of British Pottery and Porcelain Marks*, Barrie & Jenkins, 1964; *Encyclopaedia of British Porcelain Manufacturers*, Barrie & Jenkins, 1988; *Oriental Export Market Porcelain*, Granada, 1979; ed., *Staffordshire Porcelain*, Granada, 1983; *Victorian Porcelain*, Herbert Jenkins, 1961.
Honey, William, *Old English Porcelain*, Faber, new ed., 1977.
Phillip Miller and Michael Berthoud, *An Anthology of British Teapots*, Micawber, 1985.
Watney, Bernard, *English Blue and White Porcelain of the Eighteenth Century*, Faber, rev. 1973.

Samuel Alcock & Co.
c.1826-1859
Working both at Cobridge and Burslem in Staffordshire, many of the earlier teawares have only recently been identified. Best known for their range of elaborate parian wares, some shown at the Great Exhibition. Also made portrait busts and an extensive range of small animal models. Pattern numbers 1-9,999, then fractional numbers 2/ , 3/ , 4/ , etc.
Marks: Various printed marks including full name or S.A.& Co. Factory continued by Sir James Duke and nephews until 1864.
Ref: Geoffrey Godden, *Encyclopaedia of British Porcelain Manufacturers*, Barrie & Jenkins, 1988.

Lund's Bristol
1749-1751 or possibly early 1752
Benjamin Lund in partnership with William Miller continuing experiments to make porcelain begun at Limehouse in London. Eventually produced successful blue and white wares, mostly sauceboats. Transferred to Worcester in 1752. Some wares marked 'BRISTOL' in relief.
Ref: Bernard Watney, *English Blue and White Porcelain of the Eighteenth Century*, Faber, 1973.

Bristol
c.1770-1780
William Cookworthy transferred from Plymouth and perfected a hard paste formula, continued by Richard Champion. Teawares and dessert wares mostly in European neo-classical taste; particularly flower festoons favouring a green enamel. A range of figures was produced, some by John Toulouse. Exceptional flower modelling on biscuit (unglazed) plaques.
Marks: An 'X' or cross, usually in blue enamel.
Ref: F. Severne Mackenna, *Champion's Bristol Porcelain*, F. Lewis, 1947.

Bow
c.1747-1776
Factory established by 1748 in East London by a partnership including Thomas Frye. Originally styled 'New Canton', the majority of early products copied Chinese designs. Soft 'phosphatic' body with thick glaze often with uneven blue tint. Foot-rim sections are triangular and generally very shallow. Bow specialized in white glazed wares copying Chinese *blanc de chine*, and a heavy underglaze powder blue ground. A large production of figures including the work of the 'Muses Modeller' and John Toulouse, painted in slightly opaque thick enamels. Some wares were decorated at James Giles' workshop.
Marks: Generally unmarked. Early pieces can have copies of Chinese marks and an incised 'R' was sometimes used. Later wares were marked with an anchor and dagger in red enamel.
Ref: Elizabeth Adams & David Redstone, *Bow Porcelain*, Faber, 1981; Anton Gabszewicz & Geoffrey Freeman, *Bow Porcelain*, Lund Humphries, 1982.

Caughley
1772-1799
Established near Broseley in Shropshire by Thomas Turner, formerly of Worcester. Porcelain was made by 1775, closely copying Worcester. Specialized in blue-printed wares, especially heavy chinoiserie patterns. Body and glaze similar to Worcester, although it tends to have a creamy yellow tint. Early wares have unglazed bases. Foot-rim sections are square with glaze pooling under the base in greeny-yellow 'puddles'. Changed to a 'hybrid' hard paste c.1796. Firm sold to Rose & Partners of Coalport in 1799.
Marks: Many pieces were marked with the letters 'C' or 'S' either painted or printed. Sometimes with a small 'o' or 'x' alongside. Impressed mark 'Salopian' sometimes

seen on Caughley porcelain.

Ref: Geoffrey Godden, *Caughley & Worcester Porcelains*, Antique Collectors Club, 1981 (new ed.).

Chelsea
c.1744-1769

Established by Nicholas Sprimont, with finely modelled white jugs in production by 1745. Principally influenced by Meissen and subsequently early Sèvres, as well as Japanese Kakiemon and English silver shapes. Little Chinese influence. Thick white glassy glaze tending to dribble, the bases and foot-rims often ground flat after firing. Flatware fired in stilts, leaving three small scars on the bases. Paste can exhibit 'moons' (air bubbles) when held to strong light. Figures of very high quality; wide range of miniature figures; seals and scent bottles called 'toys'. The factory history is divided into periods according to the marks used.

Marks: Incised triangle *c.*1745-*c.*1749.
An anchor raised on an oval pad *c.*1749-*c.*1752.
Anchor painted in red *c.*1752-*c.*1756 (possibly later).
An anchor in gold (or brown on inferior wares) *c.*1756-*c.*1769.
Taken over by William Duesbury of Derby.
Ref: Elizabeth Adams, *Chelsea Porcelain*, Barrie & Jenkins, 1987; John Austin, *Chelsea Porcelain at Williamsburg*, Colonial Williamsburg Foundation, USA, 1977.

Chelsea – Derby
c.1770-1784

Term used to refer to wares made at Chelsea under Duesbury, and at Derby during the same period. Difficult to distinguish London from Derby products. Heavy influence of neo-classical designs.

Marks: Gold anchor continued to be used; also gold anchor and letter 'D' combined and letter 'D' below a crown, usually in blue.

Coalport
c.1795-

Porcelain first made in the 1790s beside the River Severn at Coalport, Shropshire. Took over the Caughley works in 1799. A large factory making hybrid hard paste porcelain and bone china from *c.*1815. Mostly tea and dinner services. Many wares sold in white to independent decorators. Range of flower-encrusted porcelains known as Coalbrookdale. Later, fine porcelains including jewelled wares. Pattern numbers 1-1,000; 2/1-2/999; 3/ etc., up to 7/. Usually written in gold.

Marks: Early wares usually unmarked. Impressed numeral 2 often found on plates and dishes. Printed marks including 'Society of Arts Gold Medal' from 1820. Other marks included initials 'C D' or 'C B D', for Coalbrookdale. From 1875, printed mark included 'A.D.1750', the date they claimed to have been founded.
Ref: Geoffrey Godden, *Coalport and Coalbrookdale*

Porcelains, Antique Collectors Club, (new ed.) 1981.

H. & R. Daniel
c.1826-1846

High quality porcelain made in Stoke by Henry and Richard Daniel, who had previously supervised decoration at Spode. Specialized in tea and dessert services, mostly in neo-rococo style. Rarely marked.
Ref: Michael Berthoud, *H. & R. Daniel*, Micawber Publications, 1980.

Davenport
c.1797-1887

A major factory in Longport, Staffordshire, founded by John Davenport. Hybrid hard paste porcelain made from about 1800 and bone china from *c.*1808, as well as a range of earthenwares. Tea and dessert wares and a range of rich vases, frequently marked. Later wares included a range of Imari patterns in Derby style.

Marks: Various marks combining the name Davenport and an anchor. Also printed marks, Davenport, Longport, Staffordshire.
Ref; Geoffrey Godden & Terence Lockett, *Davenport Pottery & Porcelain*, Barrie & Jenkins, 1989.

Derby
c.1748-

Several factories span two and a half centuries of porcelain making in Derby. The first wares were made under André Planche, including chinoiserie figures. William Duesbury, a London porcelain decorator became a most important figure from 1756. He bought the Chelsea factory in 1770, and finally moved to Derby in 1784. Succeeded by William Duesbury II in 1786. Specialized in figure-making and fine cabinet wares from 1770s. Major decorators included William Billingsley and superb flower and landscape painters. Factory purchased in 1811 by Robert Bloor and continued until 1848. The quality of the porcelain body declined somewhat, but standards of decoration always remained high. Famous for its Imari or Japan patterns. From 1848, new factory in King Street, Derby, which continued until 1935, specializing in copies of earlier Derby wares. A further factory was established in 1876, called Derby Crown Porcelain Co., continued after 1890 by Royal Crown Derby Co. Ltd. Specialized in use of raised gold and strong ground colours.

Marks: Early wares unmarked. Crown and letter 'D' from *c.*1770. Standard mark of crown, crossed batons, dots and 'D' used from 1780s, originally in blue, and in red after about 1800 until the 1820s. Printed crown and 'D' marks, or name of Bloor Derby used until 1848. From 1862 the King Street factory used a copy of crown, batons, and 'D' mark, with initials 'S H' for Stevenson & Hancock, and for Sampson Hancock after 1866. Derby Crown Porcelain Co. used printed crown and cypher mark. 'Royal' added

to Crown Derby in 1890.
Ref: J. Twitchett, *Derby Porcelain*, Barrie & Jenkins, 1980;
J. Twitchett and B. Bailey, *Royal Crown Derby*, Barrie &
Jenkins, 1976.

George Jones
*c.*1861-1951
Earthenware and porcelain factory in Stoke-on-Trent,
best known for majolica glazes and a range of *pâte-sur-pâte*
wares produced in the 1870s by Frederick Schenk.
Marks: 'GJ' monogram, impressed.
Ref: Geoffrey Godden, *Victorian Porcelain*, Herbert
Jenkins, 1961.

Liverpool
Very complicated history of porcelain making. Principal
factories making soft paste in the eighteenth century
include:
Richard Chaffers & Co., *c.*1755-*c.*1765; continued by
Philip Christian, 1765-1778.
Pennington: Several family members potted, including
James, John, and Seth, *c.*1763-1799.
Samuel Gilbody, *c.*1754-1761.
All made predominantly blue and white, with some
enamelled wares, mostly in Chinese style. Many different
pastes and glazes. The main Chaffers/Christian group
tends to have grey-blue tinted glaze. Foot-rim sections are
straight or undercut on inside and slanting on the outside
of the foot. Pennington was generally poorly glazed and
can appear dirty with black specks on the surface.
Marks: Virtually no Liverpool porcelain was marked in
any way.
Ref: Geoffrey Godden, *Encyclopaedia of British Porcelain
Manufacturers*, Barrie & Jenkins, 1988; Bernard Watney,
English Blue and White Porcelain of the Eighteenth Century,
Faber, 1973.

Longton Hall
*c.*1749-1760, continued at West Pans, near
Musselburgh, Scotland, *c.*1764-1777.
William Littler joined the works at Longton in
Staffordshire in 1751 and produced a wide range of
porcelains with a distinctive rustic appearance, especially
tureens and good quality figures. The factory failed, and
after a break, Littler recommenced porcelain making at
West Pans. General quality far inferior to contemporary
factories. Specialized in deep blue ground known as
'Littler's Blue'.
Marks: None at Longton Hall, 'LL' cypher at West Pans
in blue underglaze.
*Ref:*Geoffrey Godden, *Encyclopaedia of British Porcelain
Manufacturers*, Barrie & Jenkins, 1988; Bernard Watney,
Longton Hall Porcelain, Faber, 1957.

Lowestoft
*c.*1757-1799
A provincial factory in East Anglia specializing in items
decorated for the local market. Its blue and white is less
sophisticated than Worcester which it copied extensively
during the 1760s. Coloured wares in Chinese style as well
as bold flowers by the 'Tulip Painter'. Later wares in
Chinese Export style similar in design to Staffordshire.
Mostly specialized in teawares and sauceboats, while a
few rare figures and vases were made.
Marks: No factory marks, copies of Worcester and
Meissen marks on some blue and white.
Ref: Geoffrey Godden, *Lowestoft Porcelains*, Antique
Collectors Club, (new ed.), 1985; Sheenah Smith,
Lowestoft Porcelain in the Norwich Castle Museum, 2 vols.,
Norwhich Museum Service, 1975/1986.

Miles Mason
*c.*1800-1830
A dealer in Chinese porcelain, Mason became involved in
manufacture to replace stock no longer available from the
Orient. His factory at Lane Delph produced 'hybrid'
hard paste as well as bone china. Mostly with underglaze
blue printing or simple oriental patterns. Teawares and
dessert ware shapes were mostly unique to the factory and
can be fairly eccentric. Simple progressive pattern
numbers up to about 1,000. Later, the factory made
ironstone pottery with great success.
Marks: 'M.MASON', impressed on teapots or other main
pieces.
Ref: Geoffrey Godden, *Mason's China and the Ironstone
Wares*, Antique Collectors Club, 1980; Reginald Hagger
& Elizabeth Adams, *Mason's Porcelain and Ironstone*, Faber,
1977.

Minton
*c.*1796-
Initially established by Thomas Minton to make
blue-printed earthenware, the factory made porcelain
from the very end of the eighteenth century. Mostly
simple teawares until 1816. Porcelain-making revived
during the 1820s when quality and design improved
substantially. Finely detailed figures in Meissen style in
the 1830s, and Sèvres-style vases made from the 1840s.
Parian introduced in the 1840s. Many French artists were
employed in the 1850s, including Marc Louis Solon, the
greatest exponent of the *pâte-sur-pâte* technique, and
painters such as Antonin Boullemier. Pattern numbers
are simple-progressive up to 9,999, then a series of letter
prefixes were used, especially an 'A' prefix.
Marks: Crossed 'L' mark over initial 'M' used *c.*1800-
1816. Later wares rarely marked before 1840s. 'Ermine'
mark used *c.*1850, and from 1860s, the Minton name was
impressed into most wares. (Mintons after 1873). Printed
globe mark used from 1870s overglaze. Date codes
usually included.

Ref: Paul Atterbury, *Dictionary of Minton*, Antique Collectors Club, 1989; Geoffrey Godden, *Minton Pottery and Porcelain*, Barrie & Jenkins, 1968.

New Hall
c.1782-1835

An important factory at Shelton in Staffordshire catering for the more domestic porcelain market, with occasional finer and richer products. Specialized in inexpensive tea services in Chinese Export style and elegant designs using bright gold. A 'hybrid' hard paste body used until c.1814 when it was changed to bone china. Many later wares only recently recognized as New Hall. Pattern numbers used from 1 to approximately 3,500, frequently in puce with a workman's mark on earlier hybrid wares.

Marks: From about 1815, the name New Hall was occasionally printed in a black double circle.

Ref: David Holgate, *New Hall Porcelain*, new ed., Faber 1987.

Pinxton
c.1796-1813

Established in Derbyshire by William Billingsley in partnership with John Coke. Very similar paste to Derby, although decoration is mostly simple border patterns or landscapes, some attributable to Billingsley himself. Billingsley left in April 1799 and little porcelain was made there afterwards, the works continued as a decorating workshop. Some pieces bear low pattern numbers, often with a 'P' prefix. No other form of marking is now accepted as Pinxton.

Ref: C. L. Exley, *The Pinxton China Factory*, Coke-Steel, privately printed, 1963.

Plymouth
c.1768-1770

William Cookworthy's first attempts at porcelain making can appear crude and poorly fired, but these were the first hard paste wares made in England. Figures, blue and white teawares and a range of shell salts and sweetmeat dishes were made, often in white, the glaze heavily smoked. Spiral wreathing on hollow ware.

Marks: Occasionally, the chemist's sign for tin, a '2' and '4' combined, painted in blue.

Ref: F. Severne Mackenna, *Plymouth and Bristol Porcelain*, F. Lewis, 1946.

Ridgway
c.1802-1842

Various parnerships in Shelton, Staffordshire involving members of the Ridgway family produced porcelain as well as a wide range of earthenwares. Most important were John and William Ridgway, in partnership c.1814-1830 and subsequently working on their own. A small amount of ornamental wares were produced, but a wide range of tea and dinner services were made, often with very elaborate decoration. Different pattern numbers used by different family members. Generally progressive numbers up until 1815, then 2/ series up to 2/9,999, followed by 5/ series in the 1850s.

Marks: Mostly unmarked, although several elaborate marks using royal arms were used.

Ref: Geoffrey Godden, *Ridgway Porcelains*, Barrie & Jenkins, rev. ed. 1985.

Rockingham
c.1825-1842

The Brameld factory made porcelain on the estate of the Marquis of Rockingham from about 1825, specializing in tea services and ornamental vases and novelties. Many shapes have an eccentric style unique to the factory. Much confusion exists and a great many wares are incorrectly credited to the factory, especially models of sheep, poodles, and pastille burner cottages. Pattern numbers are progressive up to about 1,600, then fractional up to about 2/200. A red painted class number, 'cl 1' or 'cl 2', is frequently used on ornamental pieces.

Marks: Printed griffin with various wording, in red up until 1830, and puce thereafter.

Ref: A. and A. Cox, *Rockingham Pottery and Porcelain*, Faber, 1983; D. G. Rice, *Rockingham Pottery and Porcelain*, Barrie & Jenkins, 1971.

Spode (and Copeland)
c.1796-

Bone china body was introduced at the end of the eighteenth century, much earlier than at other factories. Plain shapes were decorated in elegant simple patterns or the richest Japan styles. Porcelain was a sideline to the vast printed pottery output, and printing was very important on early Spode porcelain.

Several name changes confuse the picture; Copeland and Garrett continued the traditions from 1833-1847, with William Copeland alone in charge from 1847. The introduction of parian from the 1840s was of enormous importance, and fine painted jewelled porcelain was made later in the Victorian period. Pattern numbers were a simple progressive series, reaching 3,000 by 1820 and over 5,000 by the Copeland and Garrett period.

Marks: A high proportion of pieces were marked with the name of the factory, usually 'SPODE' and a pattern number in red. Impressed marks are seen on earlier pieces.

Ref: Leonard Whiter, *Spode*, Barrie & Jenkins, 1970.

Swansea
c.1814-1818 and Nantgarw 1817-1819

The skills William Billingsley and Samuel Walker had learnt at Pinxton and Worcester came to fruition with the superb 'Duckegg' paste made at Swansea. Decorated to the elegant taste of the London market by some of the finest painters active at the time. Many marked pieces made attribution of unmarked pieces fairly easy, although the later 'Trident' paste body is less distinctive. Nantgarw porcelain was particularly difficult to control and was used almost exclusively for dessert plates and dishes; a large amount was decorated in London.

Marks: The name Swansea occurs impressed, painted or stencilled in red. 'NANT-GARW C.W.' (china works) was impressed. Painted Nantgarw marks are always very suspect.

Ref: W. D. John, *Swansea Porcelain*, Ceramic Book Co., 1957; Sir Leslie Joseph, *The Decoration of Swansea Porcelain*, 1989.

Wedgwood
Porcelain manufactured *c.*1812-1829 and 1878-

Josiah Wedgwood and his successors were basically potters and made surprisingly little porcelain, even though a high quality bone china body was perfected. The glaze is very white and the decoration usually tasteful. Simple progressive pattern numbers were used.

Marks: 'WEDGWOOD', stencilled in red, occasionally impressed. The factory re-introduced bone china in 1878 and used it for tea and dinner services and various ornamental wares, mostly in simple designs.

Ref: John de Fontaines, chapter on Wedgwood, *Staffordshire Porcelain*, Geoffrey Godden, ed., Granada, 1983.

Worcester
1751-

The complex history of porcelain making in Worcester covers six principal factories and has been covered extensively in this book. During the first, or Dr. Wall, period (1751-1776) the soaprock body was perfected from experiments at Bristol. Chinese decorations went hand in hand with European, with blue and white of particular importance. During the 1760s and 1770s, some porcelain was decorated in London at James Giles' workshop. The glaze has a greenish-blue tint. Foot-rim sections are triangular. Successive periods and manufactories are Davis-Flight period, 1776-1792; Flight & Barr, 1792-1804; Barr, Flight, & Barr, 1804-1813; and Flight, Barr & Barr, 1813-1840. The Chamberlain family left the main factory in 1788 and their own works ran concurrently with Flight's until 1840, when the two were combined into Chamberlain & Co. This was bought by Kerr & Binns in 1851 and became the Worcester Royal Porcelain Company in 1862.

Thomas Grainger had worked for Chamberlain and established his own factory *c.*1806, continued by the Grainger family until sold to the Worcester Royal Porcelain Co. in 1889. Other smaller factories were under the direction of Edward Locke and James Hadley later in the nineteenth century.

Marks: Up until 1760 only workmen's marks were used.

During the first period, the crescent or square marks were used on pieces with underglaze blue in their decoration. Incised 'B' marks used from 1792 until *c.*1800. After this date the majority of pieces were marked with the name of the factory. From 1862, date codes were usually present below the factory mark.

Ref: Lawrence Branyan, Neal French and John Sandon, *Worcester Blue and White Porcelain*, Barrie & Jenkins, new ed., 1989; Geoffrey Godden, *Chamberlian Worcester Porcelain*, Barrie & Jenkins, 1982; Henry Sandon, *Flight & Barr Worcester Porcelain*, Antique Collectors Club, 1978, *Royal Worcester Porcelain*, Barrie & Jenkins, 1973, *Worcester Porcelain*, Barrie & Jenkins, 1980; Simon Spero, *Worcester Porcelain: The Klepser Collection*, Lund Humphries, 1984.

Appendix 2

MARKS

It is not practical to produce here a full list of all the marks used by the porcelain makers during this period, as these would fill a volume itself as large as this book. In most cases reproducing the marks means very little, as when they are present they include the name of the factory. I have chosen to illustrate on this page some of the most frequently seen marks which do not include the name of the manufacturer. These marks, mostly painted on early porcelains, include the marks which are most frequently copied, and in illustrating these I repeat the warning that no mark can be taken purely at face value.

1. BOW – Incised mark, *c.*1750
2. BOW – Red enamel mark, *c.*1770-1775
3. BRISTOL – Blue enamel mark, 1770-1780
4. CAUGHLEY – Mark printed in blue, 1775-1785
5. CAUGHLEY – Mark printed or painted in blue, 1775-1790
6. CHELSEA – Incised mark, 1745-1748
7. CHELSEA – Red, brown or gold mark, 1752-1769
8. CHELSEA-DERBY – Gold script mark, 1770-1784
9. CHELSEA-DERBY – Blue enamel mark, *c.*1770-1784
10. COALPORT – Impressed mark, *c.*1820
11. COALPORT – Underglaze blue mark, 1825-1830
12. COALPORT – Mark in colours or gold, *c.*1851-1861
13. COALPORT – Mark in colour or gold, *c.*1861-1875
14. COPELAND – Printed mark, 1851-1885

15. DERBY – Blue or red enamel mark, c.1782-1825
16. DERBY – Bloor period; mark printed in red, c.1825-1840
17. DERBY – King Street factory, painted mark, 1861-1935
18. DERBY CROWN PORCELAIN CO. – Printed mark, c.1878-1890
19. GEORGE JONES – Printed or impressed mark, 1861-1874
20. MINTON – Mark painted in colour, c.1800-1816
21. MINTON – Impressed or printed mark, c.1845-1850s
22. PATENT OFFICE – DESIGN REGISTRATION MARK, 1842-1883
23. PLYMOUTH – Mark painted in enamel, c.1768-1770
24. SAMSON – Mark appearing on French copies of the 19th and 20th centuries
25. SWANSEA – Impressed mark, c.1816-1818

26. WEST PANS – Underglazed blue mark, c.1764-1777
27. WORCESTER – Various workmen's marks in blue c.1753-1760
28. WORCESTER – Mark painted in blue c.1760-1772
29. WORCESTER – Mark printed or painted in underglaze blue c.1760-1785
30. WORCESTER – Mark painted in blue underglaze c.1765-1775
31. WORCESTER – Mark printed in blue c.1770-1780
32. WORCESTER – Mark incorporating printed numerals 1-9, c.1785-1790
33. WORCESTER – Incised mark, c.1792-1804
34. WORCESTER – Incised mark, 1804-13; BFB – 1813-1840
35. WORCESTER – Grainger & Co., printed or impressed mark, c.1870-1885
36. ROYAL WORCESTER – Printed or impressed mark, c.1862-1890

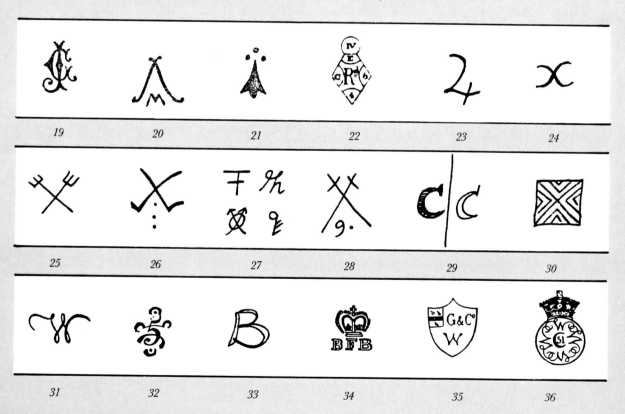

Glossary

Acid Gold
The glazed surface of the ware is etched with hydrofluoric acid and coated with burnished gold. Most popular at Minton at the end of the nineteenth century.

Aesthetic style
A further development of the Japanesque style (qv); direct copies of Japanese art adapted to suit English taste; 1880-1885.

Art Nouveau
Literally a 'new' style in art which had developed by 1900 and employed extreme asymmetry, flowing curves and plant forms. Art Nouveau had little direct influence on English porcelain.

Baroque
A style in art inspired by architectural and sculptural influences on a grand scale — shell forms and putti arranged with dramatic symmetry. Popular from the seventeenth century until it was superseded by the lighter and more frivolous rocco (qv).

Bat printing
Printing involving the use of a bat of glue to transfer the design in oil from an engraved copper plate to the surface of the ware before dusting with fine powdered colour. Bat printing produces a delicate, finely stippled effect.

Biscuit porcelain
Ware that has been fired once but not glazed; so called because of the dry, slightly rough surface. Also known as 'bisque'.

Blush Ivory
A form of decoration developed at Royal Worcester using a strongly shaded ivory and peach coloured, semi-matt ground. Much imitated during the 1890s.

Bocage
A modelled flowering tree or other leafage placed at back of a figure group as decoration, and also to add support during manufacture.

Body
A mixture of raw materials — the basic ingredients of the ware, excluding the glaze.

Bone china
A porcelain body containing up to 50 per cent animal bone and used by most English manufacturers from about 1810. The quantity of bone used can vary greatly.

Burnishing
The process of polishing gold after firing with fine sand, or hardstones such as agate or bloodstone. Patterns in the gold can be created in this way.

Calcined Bone
Animal bone reduced by heat to a powder; the ingredient of bone china (qv).

Casting
A method of forming a piece by pouring liquid clay or slip (qv) into a porous mould; any surplus is emptied out and the cast is left to dry slightly before it is removed. The alternative to press-moulding (qv).

China
A term used generally to describe any white porcelain.

China Clay
A fine white clay rich in kaolin, mined in Devon and Cornwall and used in most English china bodies.

China Stone
Partly decomposed granite rich in feldspar — a vital ingredient of porcelain, known by the Chinese as 'petuntse'.

Clobbering
Enamelling applied at a later date to add further decoration to plain white or blue and white porcelain, usually spoiling the original design.

Crazing
A fine network of tiny cracks which develop in the glaze of fired porcelain. Used intentionally by the Chinese, but an unwelcome failing in many English bone china bodies.

Creamware
A fine quality cream-coloured earthenware body made in the 1770s and 1780s in competition with porcelain.

Delftware

An earthenware with an opaque white glaze to resemble porcelain, the glaze containing tin oxide. Also called tin-glaze (or faience, *fayence* or *maiolica* in Europe).

Deutsche Blumen

Carefully painted flower decoration, developed at Meissen *c.*1740 and much copied in England.

Empire style

A development of the neo-classical style developed in France and associated with the taste of Napoleon who was made Emperor in 1804. Roman, Greek and Egyptian designs were combined on a grand scale. In England the Empire style was closely associated to the Regency style.

Enamelling

The process of decorating porcelain using colours mixed with a flux which melt into the glaze at different temperatures.

Faience or *Fayence*

The French and German equivalents of delftware (qv).

Famille Rose

A style of decoration based on Chinese porcelain painting introduced during the *Yongzheng* period in around 1730. A deep rose pink enamel features prominently in the palette.

Famille Verte

A similar style of Chinese painting with prominent use of bright green, introduced during the *Kangxi* period at the end of the seventeenth century.

Feldspar

The main component of China Stone (qv), used in most porcelain bodies.

Foot-rim

The turned base of a cup, bowl or vessel upon which it sits. Usually hand-made, the shape can be a useful guide to identification.

Gilding

Real gold applied to porcelain usually as the final embellishment. In the eighteenth century it was mixed with honey although, by the 1790s, this was replaced by mercury which produced a smoother finish. After firing, burnishing (qv) is necessary to polish the gold.

Glaze

A layer or skin of melted glass put over most ceramics to keep them clean or to enable them to hold liquids. Coloured glazes can be used as effective decoration.

Gothic style

The ornament of the medieval period which enjoyed a revival particularly in the 1830s and 1840s. The gothic style mostly influenced architecture, but had some effect on ceramics.

Groundlay

The process of applying an even background by dusting fine powdered colour onto a band of oil.

Hard Paste

A term used to describe 'true' porcelain, made from China Clay and China Stone, usually fused in a high glaze firing. Chinese and most European porcelains are hard paste, although very little was made in England.

Hybrid Paste

A term used to describe the porcelain bodies used by many English factories from the 1780s until *c.*1820. They are not hard paste in the 'true porcelain' sense but, rather, advanced forms of soft paste.

Imari

A style of decoration developed in Japan in the late seventeenth century using underglaze blue, onglaze red enamel and gold. Copied in China and widely used in England, particularly at Derby.

Indianische Blumen

A formal flower painting style developed at Meissen in the 1720s. While based on Chinese and Japanese painting, the style is much richer in colouring and design.

Japan

A rich style of decoration similar to Imari (qv), but including additional colours, particularly green. Never direct copies of Japanese porcelain, the patterns are splendid English adaptations and became popular during the Regency period.

Japanesque

A movement in art inspired by the wares and lifestyle of Japan, but becoming something of an English obsession in the 1870s and 1880s. Japanese styles were adapted to make them even more oriental in the eyes of English society.

Jewelling
A method of decorating porcelain using tiny droplets of enamel to simulate jewels. Popular in France in the nineteenth century and practised in England at Coalport and elsewhere.

Kakiemon
A class of Japanese porcelain from the late-seventeenth century much collected and heavily copied in Europe, especially at Meissen and in England at Chelsea and Bow.

Limoges Enamels
A form of decoration inspired by Medieval French enamelling, involving building up a design in layers of white enamel on a dark glazed ground.

Lithographic printing
A form of photographic litho-printing using tiny dots of colour to produce an image which is transferred to the surface of the ware. Lithographic printing was developed in the late-nineteenth century and is used extensively today.

Maiolica
The Italian name for tin-glazed earthenware or delftware, not to be confused with Majolica Ware, a form of heavily-glazed Victorian earthenware.

Moons
Tiny air bubbles trapped within the paste of Chelsea — and some other porcelain — which produces light spots when held to a strong light.

Neo-classical style
The revival of interest in formal classical styles came as a reaction against the frivolity of the rococo style. It was popular in England from the 1770s and developed into the excesses of the Regency or Empire styles in the early-nineteenth century.

Old Ivory
A form of decoration using a semi-matt ivory ground, popular at Worcester in the 1880s and 1890s; copied at Doulton and elsewhere.

Parian
A form of white porcelain containing up to 70 per cent feldspar and 30 per cent China Clay, mixed with a little crushed glass. Parian was also known as statuary porcelain and was used to make copies of marble statues. It does not need a glaze but can be used to make a creamy glazed porcelain.

Pâte-sur-pâte
A process involving building up a design by hand-painting with a white slip on a dark-coloured ground. A speciality of the Minton factory.

Pearlware
A form of white earthenware with a slight blue tint to the glaze imitating Chinese porcelain. Made in England c.170-1830.

Picturesque style
A style of painting particularly used by English water-colourists, whereby the landscape was altered to create a more attractive composition. The picturesque style was most popular at the end of the eighteenth century.

Press-moulding
A method of casting a vessel, whereby a rolled-out slab of clay is pressed into a hollow mould.

Rococo
A style in art making vigorous use of scrolls, rock and shell-forms, and asymmetry; rococo developed in the 1740s as a reaction against the more formal baroque. It was superseded by neo-classicism in the 1770s, but was revived even more strongly in the 1830s.

Saggar
A box made of fireproof clay in which porcelain vessels are placed to protect them during the firing.

Saltglaze
A type of pottery glazed during the firing as a result of a chemical reaction between the body and salt introduced into the kiln. Usually coarse and brown, some fine white saltglaze can resemble porcelain.

Slip
Clay suspended in water, used for casting (qv) and for decorating methods, such as *pâte-sur-pâte* (qv).

Soft Paste
A term used to describe 'artifical' porcelain bodies made from clay and forms of glass, fused in the biscuit (qv) kiln and subsequently given a lower glaze firing. Most eighteenth-century English porcelain is soft paste.

Spur Marks
The small scars left on the rim of a plate or saucer caused by pegs on which the piece rested during the glaze firing. This was a method used at several factories, notably Lowestoft.

Stilt Marks
A triangular arrangement of small scars, found on the base of plates or saucers which were supported on clay stilts during the glaze firing. Stilt marks are usually evident on Chelsea porcelain.

Stoneware
A hard, usually highly-fired form of earthenware made from stoneware clays. In extreme cases white stoneware can be translucent, but cannot be classed as porcelain.

Throwing
The basic method of making any ceramic vessel, with clay, on a revolving potter's wheel. Many of the plainer shapes in English porcelain are hand-thrown rather than moulded.

Transfer-printing
A design in ceramic colour is transferred from an engraved copper plate to the surface of the ware by means of a tissue-paper 'pull'. The process, developed in the 1750s, is used virtually unchanged today.

Underglaze Blue
Cobalt oxide is applied directly to the biscuit (qv) surface of the vessel and during the glaze firing reacts to seal the blue colour permanently below the glaze. Blue was the only colour which could be used satisfactorily in this way.

Wreathing
Faint spiral grooves in the surface of hard paste (qv) porcelain caused by the vessel twisting in the kiln. Wreathing can be seen on most Plymouth and Bristol hollow wares.

Index

Page numbers in italic refer to illustrations.